The Resilience Factor

How to Face Adversity, Trauma, and Tragedy Like a Superhero

Dr. Syleecia Thompson

Strategic Book Publishing and Rights Co.

Strategic Book Publishing and Rights Co., LLC
USA | Singapore
www.sbpra.net

For information about special discounts for bulk purchases, please contact Strategic Book Publishing and Rights Co. Special Sales, at bookorder@sbpra.net.

ISBN: 978-1-68235-340-0

Book Design: Suzanne Kelly
Co-editor: Chyna Parker
Foreword: Pastor Chenier A. Alston

Table of Contents

Acknowledgments..v

Foreword.. vii

Introduction.. ix

Chapter 1: Frozen at the Peak.....................................1

Chapter 2: Resilience Is Your Superpower................24

Chapter 3: You Can't Put a Band-Aid
      on a Bullet Wound 32

Chapter 4: Turning into Wonder Woman.................40

Chapter 5: The Hero's Journey 55

Chapter 6: Leaving the Rat Race...............................64

Chapter 7: More Money, No Problems......................72

Chapter 8: A Purposeful Pandemic...........................83

Your Resilience Factor Journal 91

About the Author 127

Acknowledgments

Thank you, God, for giving me the strength and courage to finish this book. I am forever humbled by the way you have protected me. I would like to thank my family and friends for pushing me throughout this journey. It meant the world to me. To my doctors, nurses, nutritionist, trainers, therapist, and surgeons who have single-handedly changed the trajectory of my life: I appreciate you. I must also acknowledge all of the bad experiences and traumas I've encountered that made me stronger: thank you. Thank you to all of the people who may have not had my best interest at heart or who betrayed me: thank you. It is these encounters, circumstances, and trials that built my resilient mindset and pushed me to overcome. I want to send love, light, and encouragement to all of the women and men around the world who have suffered a loss of any kind, especially those who have lost babies. We are a special group of angel moms and dads. To my very exclusive class of superheroes, breast cancer survivors, you are brilliant, resilient, and vibrant. You are worthy of life. In the end, we are judged not by who we are and the money we've made, but by the impact we have left on others and this world.

Foreword

Life is often compared to a rollercoaster in which one minute you are up, then in the next minute you are down. In order to survive life's series of ups and downs you must be resilient. Resilience is that internal factor that gives you the power or ability to remain in your true form and position while being pulled, pressed, and persecuted by some of life's most difficult problems. This is what Syleecia has demonstrated throughout her life while going through a series of challenging events. I watched her remain resilient in the face of adversity. She became the hero in her own story and an inspiration to those who find themselves facing life's most difficult moments. Her story is real and powerful, transparent, and inspiring. I remember there were times when she could have easily given up and thrown in the towel, but her resilience drove her to a place in her life where the moniker that now hangs over it is that of, "unbroken and undefeated." I can still recall the day when I spoke with her and she informed me that she was battling breast cancer. What I was expecting to hear were the sounds of hopelessness coming from her but instead what I heard were the words from the heart of a warrior destined to win. She was in pain and immense discomfort, but she remained resilient. That is what you will read in this book. You will read about a woman of courage, a woman who was determined to win despite the odds that were stacked against her. You will read about a woman whose resilient faith gave credence to words penned by the Apostle Paul when he said, "And let us not grow weary in well doing, for in due season you will reap a harvest, if you do not give up (Galatians 6:9)" Syleecia reaped a harvest of success because she remained resilient which now serves as a successful teaching tool for all of us. So, as you read this book, you will be inspired to become the resilient factor in your own story regardless of the adversities you may be facing. Enjoy the journey.

Pastor Chenier A. Alston

Introduction

Life is unpredictable. Trauma is inevitable. In life, sometimes trauma gets frozen at the peak. This means that at the highest point of your pain oftentimes you get stuck there and moving on toward the healing process either never happens or takes a significant amount of time. Everyone faces trauma. Trauma is the experience of severe psychological or physical distress following any terrible or life-threatening event. People develop emotional disturbances such as extreme anxiety, anger, sadness, survivor's guilt, or PTSD (Post Traumatic Stress Disorder). Trauma is extremely common. We will all face it at some point in our lives. It's an emotional response that often sets us back. Trauma can be physical or emotional and is different for everyone. Our history of trauma may make us so immune to tragedy that we develop a high tolerance for pain, especially emotional pain.

I am going to be honest. Yes, right at the beginning of this book. Let me just tell it all. I have suffered from PTSD. I have experienced deep depression. I have filed for bankruptcy. I have lost all of my money and gained it back. I have had a 500 credit score and a 720 credit score. I have been suicidal. I have had an abortion. I have suffered a stillbirth. I have survived cheating boyfriends. I have been married and divorced. I have been diagnosed with Stage 1 breast cancer. I have beat cancer. Right now, as I type this sentence, I am living through the coronavirus pandemic.

One can say I have experienced my share of trauma. I have been frozen and stuck. I have been in fight-or-flight mode many times over the course of my forty-something-plus years of living. I feel like I've been through it all and seen it all. I've dealt with stress on various levels, so I truly understand the impact it has on people. I also know it's not easy to bounce back. Trauma and stress can be overwhelming. It can sometimes feel like you will never make it through. It often seems like it's too powerful to overcome. As a human being, your first impulse is to give up, but what sets you apart from most people who do give up is your willingness to stay and fight through it. Sometimes we feel like we can't defend ourselves against the trauma, but I am living proof that is a lie. We are equipped with the tools led by our faith to conquer our most traumatic experiences.

I want you to see yourself in me and know that you can overcome anything that life throws your way. My story is special to me, but it is not unique. There are millions of people who have faced pregnancy loss, breast cancer, financial woes, relationship hardships, and personal defeats. I am just a person who decided not to let it define me or break me. My story proves that what many think of as impossible is actually possible. My story is a story of resilience. I am resilient. You are resilient too, and I am going to prove it to you by the time you finish reading this book.

Healing is a part of your journey. Resilience is your saving grace. The resilience process can heal wounds.

Resilience can break through your traumas. When faced with adversity, you discover who you are and what you are capable of overcoming. This positions and prepares you for a purposeful and bountiful life. We should look at our journey in life through the lens of resiliency to have a more fruitful, productive, and guilt-free life. I want to take you on a journey in this book. I want to share my life's story. I will share my losses and gains with you, including my love life, lessons learned, and how certain relationships transformed me into the person I am today.

I lived in fear for the first half of my life. Fear of not finding love. Fear of loss. Fear of not fulfilling my true purpose and passion. I feared flying. I feared heights. I was even afraid of fear. I was afraid to die. I was so afraid of death because I wasn't truly living. The moment I realized you can't spend your whole life in fear was when death drew close. That moment was having a stillborn baby. I had a life die inside of me. There was nothing more devastating that I had faced in my life. As a woman, carrying a life inside of you is the greatest gift on earth. Consequently, realizing that a life inside of you has died is the greatest curse on earth. With death so close to me, I realized there was an art to living, and fear of everything was trying to break me.

The art of living is truly defined by how many times you bounce back, get up, and keep pushing through all of the setbacks faced in life. It sounds so simple and cliché, but life is truly about your resilience. It is not about how much money you have or acquire. It's not about the material things you own or the men and women you marry. It's about how you get back up after feeling like life would keep you down. Living your life to the fullest can only be achieved by your ability to be strong and live resiliently.

There is one constant force in this thing we call life, and that is the amount of negative, unstructured, and dangerous obstacles that will be thrown our way. It is human nature to look at successful people and believe, "Oh, they have it made," or think, "They probably don't have any problems." These statements are far from reality or truth. Life, loss, love, and learning valuable lessons are inevitable, regardless of age, race, ethnicity, or background. Rich or poor, no man or woman is exempt from suffering, misfortune, death, loss, or pain. We all have mountains to climb in life. Once I realized that my journey was going to be plagued with problems, confrontation, pain, hurt, disappointments, and conflict—and there was nothing I could do about it for the most part—I developed a sense of calmness about certain obstacles that came my way. I began to focus on solutions to every problem encountered. I was learning to become, with each battle, a tower of strength through resilient living. I realized that I had a high tolerance for emotional pain, and that this was not right. I had to work on that part of my life. Just because I could take a lot of trauma and tragedy didn't mean I had to.

You will discover throughout this book that I have encountered a lot of losses and setbacks. I wrote this book to share my story and help other people heal, with nuggets of information and inspiration shared throughout. I'm not going to tell you that you will be able to conquer every trial in the most triumphant or graceful way. I will tell you that you are tough, strong, and powerful. I will tell you that you can overcome and pull through anything and emerge better than you were prior to your trauma. After reading this book, you will believe you should never give up. You should not let bad habits or bad experiences drain your progress toward a resilient mindset. This is not who we are as humans. By God's design, we are entitled to a bountiful life and required to be the best version of ourselves. Your hardest times will often lead to your greatest moments. God does not want you to give up.

CHAPTER 1

Frozen at the Peak

Life is full of unpredictable traumas.

Born on Christmas Day. I guess you can say I entered this world in an unpredictable way. I was a gift to my parents. I was born December 25, 1972, around six p.m. in Harvey, Illinois (a suburb outside of Chicago). My mother loves to tell the story of me interrupting her Christmas dinner. She was pregnant and stuffing her face at the dinner table at my grandparents' home when her water bag broke. Oops! My fault, sorry, Ma. She wasn't expecting me to come that day. Even the process of giving birth teaches us that we can't control life's ultimate path for us. It's unpredictable. It humbles us and humors us in ways we could never imagine. I believe coming into the world this way was a sign for an incredible journey to come.

Being born on Christmas Day had its advantages and disadvantages as a child. I was showered with gifts for my birthday and for Christmas. My mother likes to remind me of this every holiday. But as an adult those double gifts turned into singles. As we mature, our needs and wants change, so the expectation of a bunch of gifts should decrease. It was a day of celebration, and it was also a religious holiday. I had to look at it as sharing a birthday with Jesus Christ. The power behind this notion has followed me throughout my life.

I have many amazing Christmas memories with me, my sisters, and the rest of our family. My mom and dad always provided for us. They spoiled us. I had two sisters growing up in my household as a young child: Sylette was the oldest, and Syleena was the youngest. I am a middle child. We were very close. We were inseparable. We shared many things in common such as Barbie dolls, board games, playing school, and toys. We would wake up very early on Christmas Day every year at like three a.m. and prepare to go downstairs because we knew Santa (our parents) had brought us everything we wanted and more. This is what I dreamt of for my son or daughter: great holidays shared with family and the feeling that Christmas brought. It was the best time of my life! I was like any other kid who was elated to see the lights, the decorations, and, of course, the gifts. The experiences I had as a child around the holidays helped shape me as an adult. I developed a sense of community, working together with others, and the joys of sharing moments with those you care most about.

As a teenager, I wondered what it would be like to have a daughter. My goal in life was to always do the exact opposite of what my parents would do. Honestly, I think that should be everyone's goal. When you know better, you should do better. But as a child I always thought about having a little girl, sort of like a mini me. I've always wanted to have only one child. That has been my goal since forever. One child and that was it. I don't know why, though. I grew up in a household with two sisters, a half-brother, and two half-sisters. My father had three other children with his first wife. We were closest to one of his daughters, Michelle. I loved Michelle. She was the best big sister a girl could have.

I was a different type of teenager. I hated high school. It felt like torture attending each year. High school was unfulfilling to me; I can recall not being interested in any subjects. I graduated early just so I could go to college to escape my parents' home. They were too strict. After Sylette, my older sister, got pregnant at seventeen, they turned into jail wardens. It was a jailhouse on Ashland Avenue in Harvey, Illinois. My dad would pull guns out and lay them on the kitchen table when boys would come by to visit us. So, needless to say, there was no freedom. I think that is what caused me to be very withdrawn in high school. I couldn't take it, so I wanted out, and college was that outlet to escape.

I went to Southern Illinois University at Edwardsville. College was an incredible experience for me. My first day on campus taught me a lesson. I remember showing up and meeting my roommates for the first time. As I walked into the apartment (we had apartments, not dorms), I remember looking at my roommates and saying, "Lord Jesus, help me." They were so opposite of each other and so opposite of me. One of them was a young white girl who had the typical California swag. The other roommate was straight St. Louis (that's what I will call her, St. Louis). Gold teeth and all, she was a firecracker. She was a twenty-year-old black woman who had already been on campus for three years when we arrived. She was older than both of us. I walked in

3

and said "Hello," and I just remember the California roommate saying "Hi!" with great cheer, and then St. Louis looked at me with a nonchalant attitude as she sat on the couch and didn't flinch. I knew trouble was ahead. The white girl left first because she couldn't take St. Louis. After the white girl left, they moved a Chinese woman in. The cultural differences made things worse. St. Louis later got kicked out of the apartment because she smoked weed every day, and neither I nor the Chinese girl could take it. I don't do weed or smoke. She violated our space and refused to change.

College matured me. It taught me determination, a good work ethic, how to deal with others, ethnicity, cultural differences, sisterhood, vigor, defeat, failure, and success. I loved every minute of it. It was probably a period in my life where I started to learn who I was going to be. I joined a sorority, Zeta Phi Beta (the best sorority on earth), and met a lot of great people. This is also where I met my ex-husband. He was a man I later would loathe and divorce, but nonetheless I met him in college. I graduated with a Bachelor of Science in economics, and shortly after graduation moved to Tampa, Florida, to live with my boyfriend, who later turned into my husband. He was a very sweet and kind guy, but he was just not motivated or passionate about anything. We were not equally yoked. Living in Tampa, I learned so much about myself and him that later on I realized we were not compatible. The weather was awesome, and the vibe was laid back, but I was really unhappy living there. It was starting to change me.

Before leaving Tampa, I received my master's degree in business, and that was the moment I realized

I wanted to teach. I stayed in Florida for four and a half years and later moved back to Chicago to live in the south suburbs. I got married despite knowing it wasn't gonna last and worked extremely hard to finish my doctorate, and then I started working in entertainment and teaching part-time at the local college. I got married in 2001 and divorced in 2004. During that time I made sure I would not have a baby by a man with whom I was not equally yoked. I just couldn't do it. So, I put off having children to focus on my education and career. You know how sometimes you do things that you know are wrong in your spirit but still pursue them? God gives you a truckload full of signs, but either your ego or hard head keeps you holding on to poor decisions. This was one of those times. I learned valuable lessons because of the financial and emotional issues I faced during this marriage. I got into tax debt and other financial situations that stemmed from my ex-husband. This was a loss that I was able to get over emotionally, but not financially. It took me many years to dig out of the hole he put me in. I have a very strange way of trusting men a little too much; I guess you can say this is part of my personality that needed correction. After my divorce, I started to come into my true self. I was free to do many things I couldn't do trapped in that marriage. I started to travel, love more of the things I had a deep interest in, such as working out and reading more, and I learned to see the world for what it was. I started to be me. It was so exhilarating.

My sister Syleena signed her first record deal in 1998 with Jive Records under the stage name of Syleena Johnson. She recorded her first album, and three years later it was released. Syleena's first tour was the TP2.com tour with R. Kelly in 2001, and I remember bringing my husband at the time on that tour. I remember it being not a fun time for any of us. Syleena was having issues with her husband at the time, and I was having issues with mine. It was interesting, to say the least, but we pushed through it. I just remember us leaving them in the hotel and escaping to go places without them.

The tour was successful and my first glimpse into the world of music. Syleena opened up for R. Kelly, and she was basically able to establish herself in the world of rhythm and blues and position herself as a powerhouse voice in the industry. However, she began to search for another business manager, and I took on that position in 2002 after the tour ended. I started to manage my sister's finances in 2002, and from that point on I was tied to her career. I created my company and started to think like an entrepreneur. I later became her road manager and then her music manager. You never know what opportunities God will give you in the midst of uncertain times. These moments always add an extra element of required focus and spiritual awareness.

With this new role, I was still working corporate jobs, teaching, and doing entrepreneurial activities on the side. It was a fun time in my twenties! The music business brought a unique experience to me. It showed me the dark side of music and the creative side of the business. I learned the financial accounting process as her business manager. Balancing the books with her accountant, paying her bills, monitoring expenses and income was not an easy task to do for your sister. You had to be extra careful and cautious.

As her career progressed, I got more and more active inside of her infrastructure. By 2003, she was on her second album, touring and dealing with all the drama that came with the record label. Eventually, I became her road manager, and a very exciting opportunity came to us with the recording of her third album. She got the opportunity to work with Kanye West, who was also a Chicago native. They recorded a song together for her third album, and he needed her to record a song for his first album. This hook became one of his biggest and best-selling songs, *All Falls Down*. This song gave us the opportunity to travel and tour with him in support of his first album, *The College Dropout*. It was an exciting time. It was very different from her first touring experience with R. Kelly. So, when we got to tour in 2004 with Kanye West, I was in a different place mentally and professionally.

From about 2003 to 2008, we accomplished a lot. We learned the business of music and began to gain a sense of independence. We closed several record deals with various labels, released an independent project, and secured a few television placements. However, in 2008, I knew Chicago was not the place for me. It just felt like my time was up there and I had hit a wall. I was starting to feel complacent and confused about my direction. I was single with no children and uneasy about my situation. I was not happy. So, I started to apply for college teaching positions out of state. There was one college that called me within days of my applying, and I will never forget how fast I got that position. They were so nice on the phone interview, and in person they were even better. I moved to New York City one month after getting the job. It was super exciting. I took a lot of chances and I've never been afraid to create opportunities for myself. I believe this has given me a foundation for strength building.

I had to figure out my living situation quickly. I had a mortgage in Chicago, so I had to figure that out as well as how I was going to move to another state within a matter of weeks. The way I got my apartment in New York City was crazy. Syleena had a show with Fantasia in the summer of 2004, and I met Fantasia's bodyguard. We began a friendship and talked on the phone frequently. He casually mentioned to me he knew someone who needed to sublet his apartment in NYC, and I said that I needed a place. He hooked me up with the person, Gavin Gregory (who is a really good friend of mine to this day), and that place later became my apartment. It was so cute and adorable. Gavin was a neat freak. I moved to New York City on September 29, 2008, with everything in my Chrysler Sebring convertible. Life is truly unpredictable.

Sylette and I drove from Chicago to New York on Sunday, September 28, 2008, and slept overnight in Pennsylvania somewhere. We were super tired because we had gone to a party at R. Kelly's house the night before. I didn't care because I wanted to party one last time before I moved to New York City. We drove on three hours of sleep. Anyway, we finally arrived on that Monday, and I had never seen the apartment. The superintendent let me in, and I loved it. I was so worried to move to this city and did not even know how the place looked. But I stepped out on faith. The day I moved in was the same day I started teaching. I know, crazy. So, we unloaded the car and found the nearest train to hit the city so I could begin teaching. Sylette stayed in NYC for two weeks until I became acclimated to the town. I lived in Harlem. I loved it. The scenery and the people reminded me of something out of a movie. The day Sylette left to go back to Chicago I decided to dress up and hit one of the local lounges. I went to Moca Lounge in Harlem because that was a popular spot. That is where I met the father of my child. The child I would later lose.

As a college professor and entertainment manager, I have always tried to merge the two. I teach a music business class at Berkeley College, and I often bring my strategic planning skills into the entertainment world. It works. It fits. I love doing both. They both fulfill me. I am an educator at my core. At times, the music business is stressful. There are times when I despise it. There are times when I wish I didn't have to do it. Honestly, my sister's talent keeps me going. She has one of the best voices of our time. That is what motivates me. I'm also motivated by watching others learn, grow and transform so having multiple skill sets fulfills me.

After giving birth to a stillborn baby, I wanted out of the industry so bad. There are times I still want out and barely holding on. I don't know what is going to keep me thriving but I do know the thrill and experience is worth it.. What I've learned in life is that there are different types of love. I love my career and the experience that I've obtained over the last twenty years. It's been a hell of a ride. I love the music business for the creation and performance parts of it. I hate everything else. I pray every day for strength. There are times I feel resilient, and there are times I feel defeated. Ultimately, part of my resilience factor was built from the entertainment industry.

As the years passed by, my focus was on teaching at Berkeley College and running my company, DYG Management Group, LLC. In 2011, Nicci Gilbert from Brownstone reached out to us and asked Syleena to be a part of R&B Divas. That was a cool time in our lives. It was TV, and it was going to change things up. We were excited and grateful for the opportunity. The music industry has always been a passion of mine. I just never cared for the politics and bullshit that came with it. The music industry is not friendly to women. What I mean by that is that the music industry punishes you for being a woman. You can't get emotional (or you are considered weak), you can't have a baby (or you are considered unfocused or may lose your appeal), you can't get a husband (or you are considered not positioned to get results), and you can't speak your mind (because you are considered bossy). All of these things create a stressful environment.

During my pregnancy, I would have never expected to be faced with such extreme stress, pressure, and decision-making. It was probably one of the most difficult "music business" years I've had in the twelve years that I have been in it. I just don't know how women have babies or families in this industry. It's not conducive to peace. You have to be strong-minded and disciplined. You have to stand firm on what you believe in and stick to your principles. You must always remember that you come first before the industry, your clients, or your career. When I say "you," I truly mean "you" as a human being with feelings, emotions, and a body that must be cared for.

In 2013, I put together Syleena's first European tour. This tour represented all that I'd worked for in the music business. It was hosted in three main parts of Europe: France, Holland, and cities across the UK. It was an opportunity that created a success story for my company. Touring and booking are very important to managers in the entertainment business. They give you leverage and keep your artist relevant. So, when the tour came together I was elated. Amsterdam was the first stop on the tour. Amsterdam, home of marijuana! Well, it is a beautiful place. I planned this tour for six months. The time was finally here. Tickets booked, and we were ready to go. Syleena and Amir, her bodyguard, met me at the airport. I love traveling but hate flying.

I want to take you on a journey toward motherhood. The journey begins with love. Love changes you. Sometimes for the better. Sometimes for the worse. I have always wanted to experience the unconditional love that you receive from a child. That has always been a desire of mine. Not only were we traveling to Europe to experience new cultures, but I was embarking upon a new reality at the beginning of the trip. This was a bittersweet trip. I found out I was pregnant in Amsterdam. Syleena and Amir were with me. They convinced me to go get a pregnancy test because I was a few days late coming on my menstrual cycle. I thought I was late on my period because of the traveling and long flight. I found a little store in Amsterdam that sold pregnancy tests. It was interesting because the language on the test kit was in Dutch, but I knew that the plus or minus signs would be similar to a US test. I couldn't understand the writing on the package at all! I took the test in the bathroom of an Indian restaurant, and within minutes it was positive. I couldn't believe it. I was happy but scared because I was in a foreign country and far away from my boyfriend, at that time.

I was pregnant at forty years old. In the beginning, I was beyond ecstatic. There was a life growing inside of me, an experience that was special beyond belief. A connection that many don't get the chance to experience. When I returned from the European tour, I was feeling like I would finally get that mini me. The joy I experienced was indescribable. I had put off a family for so long, because of my career, that once I found out I was pregnant at forty years old I knew it would be a new beginning and bring great change from the life I was living.

I started preparing to be a mom. When I found out I was having a girl, I named her Nikeeya Nichelle Fisher. Syleena's middle name is Nikeeya, and Sylette's middle name is Nichelle. I gave her a nickname too: Keeya. I painted her room sunshine yellow. I prepared my mind and started reading books on motherhood and caring for children. I was mentally and physically preparing every day. Things turned around quickly, though, because at my second doctor's visit I was informed of news that would change the trajectory of my pregnancy. At seventeen weeks, complications started. Doctors noticed that at the seventeen-week mark, she was still the weight of a baby at the fifteen-week mark. They decided to keep a close watch on her and me.

As I was going along with my pregnancy, she just wasn't growing. I was going to several doctors' appointments, but the doctors didn't know what was going on, and it made me upset. They told me I wouldn't make it past twenty weeks. No mother wants to hear that their child growing inside of them won't make it. It was one of the toughest times for me that really should have been one of the happiest moments of my life.

I tried to take control by being proactive and needed to know why she wasn't growing at a healthy rate. I did everything I could to get her to grow, taking whatever advice they gave me, trying different diets, and watching my blood pressure. I never smoked in my life and was a very casual drinker prior to being pregnant, so that wasn't the issue. I tried acupuncture, and I was taking every precaution I could. I was diagnosed with IUGR, an intrauterine growth restriction, meaning a baby doesn't grow to a normal weight during pregnancy. Some of the causes of IUGR are placenta abnormalities, high blood pressure in the mother, infections, abuse of alcohol, or frequent smoking. I didn't have any of those issues. My mind was racing trying to find the cause of the diagnosis. If she grew to at least one pound, she would have been premature and just stayed at the hospital to continue to grow. Ultimately, that was my mission. Looking back on it now, I likely had problems with inflammation and circulation, and I'm even wondering if it was an autoimmune issue or my weight.

In the end, this was not enough to save her, and it took a toll on my mental health and my body. I lost my baby at seven months through a stillbirth (the birth of an infant that has died in the womb). It was completely devastating. In a routine checkup, the ultrasound technician was running the machine along my stomach before telling me that she would be right back. I was in there alone, freaking out because something made me believe that things were not okay. The doctor came into the examining room, and not the ultrasound tech, so I knew something was off. This is when my nightmare started.

Once a baby dies inside of you, they have to induce labor. I was taken to the hospital immediately and set up in a room to give birth. I called my sisters and my boyfriend, Omar, who left work early to come to the hospital. Syleena would later fly into New York to be with us during the delivery. With my epidural in, it was time to start a process that ended in an extreme manner. I wasn't dilating and ended up breaching with her body first instead of her head. Eventually, they were able to remove her.

My daughter's due date was supposed to be December 4th. I loved the month of December. It was my favorite month of the year, and now that Keeya's due date was December 4th I was even more ecstatic about the day. I had everything planned out for Keeya's first Christmas. The toys, the games, and the dolls. I was overjoyed to know that I was having a girl. I knew in my heart I was having a girl. And oh did I have plans for her. Outfits, room color, and school clothes were all planned out for the next eighteen years. I even had visions of us taking the train on long-distance trips together. I loved the train, so I was prepared to take Keeya with me to experience this passion of mine. Girl time getaways on Amtrak.

We left the hospital on September 19, 2013, at 1:30 p.m. I remember Omar rolling me out of the hospital room in a wheelchair, and I remember thinking, *Is this really my life?* I was in complete shock. What was the lesson? I had no idea how to cope, move on, or survive. At this point, I just didn't understand what I was supposed to take away from this nightmare as a lesson. I was confused, dazed, in pain, and crying. The nerve damage in my leg was shooting through my entire body. However, the mental pain outweighed the physical pain. Sure, I had cramps and nerve damage in my leg, but mentally I was fucked up. Beyond anyone's imagination. I didn't know how I would survive. The only understanding I had at that point was that I lost a baby whom I wanted so badly. The pain of losing a child is the most horrific pain anyone could endure. I'm sure there are other setbacks, disasters, or horrific pains in this world, but for me the pain of losing our baby who grew inside me for seven months was mortifying. I was twenty-eight weeks when I delivered. The hardest thing in life is to carry a child inside the womb and lose them. No woman should have to suffer this loss.

A few months after the stillbirth, I read her autopsy. I felt sick to my stomach. Her head was decapitated, which is how they took her out of me. I wanted to just get in my bed and sleep forever after reading that. It felt like I was taking blow after blow with no light at the end of the tunnel. Thirty hours of labor while in pain with a deceased baby inside of me made me want to just give up. The pain of going through this labor and the pain of losing her were all too much. I was at my lowest point. A life was lost within me, and my life itself was shattered. It felt like there was no bouncing back from this.

A mother will never get over losing a child. It stays with her forever. A baby is the only person in the world who hears the mother's heartbeat on the inside. They are the closest to the heart of a mother. However, the father is also damaged. A piece of him dies as well. Dads hurt too. They hurt for themselves, the baby, and the mother. Men are considered the warrior, head of the household, and the support system. Society expects them to bounce back and be strong for everyone. When you lose a baby, you realize how strong men and fathers can be in the face of adversity. Omar was super strong. I've never seen anything like it. When he cried in the hospital, it wasn't a cry of weakness. He cried because he had lost his daughter. It was so tough for me to see him cry. I hated to see that. I think we learn to love people more when we go through shattering events with them. This stillbirth enabled me to view him in a different light. For many, that may seem strange, but for me it's real. Eventually, Omar and I broke up five years later. It just didn't work out. That was another loss I had endured, but it was easier to cope with.

When I came home, I was visited by my mother and my sister Sylette. They came to stay with us for a week or so. My mother cooked and cleaned and went down to the neighborhood deli to buy scratch-offs. She was determined to hit the lottery while staying with us in New York City. Ha! I just remember crying every day, all day. So many people sent flowers to our home. ThinkFactory Media, my sister Michelle, Berkeley College, my aunts, uncles and a few others sent flowers and cards. I felt like truly someone had just died. I realized that when you have a stillborn baby, you are in an exclusive club of mothers who have babies born into heaven. I never thought this would be my story.

The emotional roller coaster you are on when you lose a baby is quite frustrating. Crying happens every day, all day. Flashbacks, regret, guilt, blame, and sadness occur as well. I blamed myself for a long time. It was part of the suffering I encountered. When I came home from the hospital, I had to deal with physical, emotional, and financial pain. I was forced to speak with insurance companies, handle disability claims, and set up all my doctors' appointments. No one did it for me. At the time, my boyfriend was there for support. However, he had to go back to work, which left me alone in the house. Very few people offered to help me with anything, and how could they? They didn't know what to do.

However, looking back on that time I think I would have accepted some help from people to assist with calling insurance companies and fighting for my disability. It was exhausting. I can't even believe I went through that type of agony alone. My health insurance company was amazing. The people there helped me in every type of way imaginable. But my disability company (who I shall not name), who was holding my short-term disability policy payment, treated me poorly, and they were a complete disaster. They denied my claim beyond six weeks. They felt I had more than enough time to recover and get back to teaching. This was so crazy. Imagine losing a baby and having to go out on disability and then fighting to get paid while you're on disability. It was terrible. They put profits over people, and it wasn't that much money that I was owed, so that even made it more ridiculous. However, I got an attorney to pursue it and contacted Governor Cuomo's office, then I was able to get paid. Governor Cuomo's office was absolutely amazing.

Losing hurts. No one wants to lose anything. I've lost boyfriends, cars, homes, shoes, friends, cell phones, and many other items, but never have I lost a child. My life flashed before my eyes when they told me there was no heartbeat. I began journaling after losing the baby. Here is an excerpt:

I'm in a crappy mood today. My menstrual cycle started and that is one more reminder that I'm not pregnant. I have postpartum, I am grieving, and I have terrible cramps. No one should have to suffer like this. It's pure torture. People keep telling me "everything happens for a reason" and "God has a bigger plan for your life" but all I want to do is go crawl in a hole somewhere and die. I'm praying every day. I'm praying for mental peace and healing. I'm frustrated. How long does this last? Days, months or years? My thoughts have been so

*negative that all I can do is pray. I don't want
to be a negative person.*

Another excerpt from my journal:

*Today, I feel a little stronger. Something in
me wants to fight. Fight for my sanity. Fight
for my peace of mind. Fight for Keeya. Fight
for my family. I just want to stand up and fight
and be strong. I feel like I want to try to have
another baby. I feel like I want to focus, plan
and strategize. I don't know why I feel like this.
I have been down for so long.*

Writing can help with the healing process. I wanted
to share some of my journal excerpts to show you I was
in a very dark place. You can tell from the writings that
I was hurting, and I was struggling to get through some
tough moments. You can also tell from the second
excerpt that I had moments of resilience. I didn't want
to just share my bounce back, or my comeback, without
letting people see the actual hurt and pain that came
from this trauma. I was journaling almost every day.
I won't share the rest of the excerpt with you because
it was just too dark and, looking back, I wasn't always
the most positive person during that time, which was
to be expected. There is no time limit on grief. I had to
understand that, and writing my thoughts down proved
that. I journaled for more than a year, and with each
day the writing got more and more positive.

Going forward, I learned a lot over the next six
years. I closed some pretty major deals, lost seventy

pounds, and moved into my own place. In the summer of 2018 I was transitioning out of a nine-year relationship and learning to live on my own. I was finally at a place where I accepted the pregnancy loss, but now I was experiencing a relationship loss. The loss of a nine-year relationship did affect me, but not as bad as some of the other traumatic events I had faced. When you break up with someone it's a constant reminder that maybe you weren't good enough, smart enough, or pretty enough. All of these things went through my mind, but ultimately I had to understand that people come into your life for a season and a reason. Looking back on that relationship was so I could experience my pregnancy loss, which ultimately shaped and created the woman I am today. Now, of course, there are other lessons to be learned from being in a nine-year relationship with no end result or hope of marriage, but I'd like to sum it up as life. Life is unpredictable. It is what it is. Just take your time when dealing with a broken heart.

My business acumen and entrepreneurial skills were getting strong. I started my coaching and brand strategy program and began to help people start businesses and develop their brands. My entertainment business was booming. I closed deals in television, film, and brand partnerships. Some of my accomplishments included a film called *Couples Therapy*, a record label deal with eOne Entertainment/Nashville, over thirty television interview placements for my clients, several tours, a speaking tour for myself, and solidifying Syleena's *Sister Circle*, a national talk show. In addition to these things, I launched a clothing collection, The Christian

Dion Collection, a few albums, *Rebirth of Soul* and *Woman* by Syleena Johnson, and Dr. Ivan Hernandez's tour for his book, *Courage to Continue*. I was also able to secure European, US, and South Africa tours for Syleena. All of these projects gave me joy and fulfillment.

Building relationships with partners in South Africa was another highlight for me. Syleena has toured the country several times, each time allowing us the opportunity to learn about their conditions, understand their struggles, and truly find out how resilient we are as a people. South Africa is an amazing place. I think all black people who live in America should visit Africa at some point in their lives. I would recommend going to South Africa first. It has the deepest and richest culture and symbolisms that helped me understand that resilience truly is in my DNA.

While working in entertainment, I was faced with a lot of setbacks and financial woes. It wasn't always nice and pretty. When you work in the music industry, everyone sees the glitz and the glamour. They see the music videos, the bottle service at the clubs, the fancy clothes and cars, but they rarely see the steps of anyone's pain behind the scenes. You have to be resilient if you're going to work in the music business. That's a no-brainer. If you're not, you will get eaten alive. So I think I learned to have tough skin for the most part as it related to my business life, and I think that impacted my personal life as well. I've dealt with shady people in the business and people that just were not honest. I learned a lot about the human race. There were many times I wanted to quit the music industry and maybe just go back to a corporate job. But my passion and purpose for helping people, for building brands, and for working in music was stronger and greater. I also think because I was my sister's manager played a big role as well, and it allowed me to continue to push forward. If she wasn't going to give up, I couldn't give up either— and vice versa. The music business punishes you for being a woman. So, you have to be extra tough with a shrewd sense of survival. As women, we were born resilient. It's not until we are tested that we realize we have strength beyond measure.

I felt pretty good about my career path, but it was my personal journey that weighed the heaviest on me. I wasn't happy. I wasn't living my best life. Although on the outside it looked like it. Being a black woman in your forties, single with no kids, can be frustrating. It can be demeaning and depressing. It is also a time of growth and self-discovery. There are days you feel amazing and days you feel drained.

Summer of 2018 was a game changer for me. I think this was the summer I poured myself into my work, not remembering that stress is not good for your body either. During this year, I went on a speaking tour and booked twelve speaking engagements. I love speaking, sharing, and educating other women. This was the period after leaving a nine-year relationship. I should have taken a break and sought therapy. But I didn't.

The summer of 2019 was when my life changed forever. This summer I would get a diagnosis like no other. I was diagnosed with Stage 1 breast cancer (later I discovered after removal of the tumor it was

Stage 2) at the height of my teaching career and with many successes under my belt as an entrepreneur. I started working on a clothing collection launch, which was an exciting time for me. I also worked on new projects such as branding with a dermatologist, Dr. Dele-Michael, documentary filming with Miss Black USA, Syleena's new album project, and training with four new entrepreneurs. The summer was filled with new opportunities and strong business ventures amidst this diagnosis. I'll take you through my breast cancer journey later on in this book.

If I could look back on my life and change what I've gone through in the past, I could honestly say I wouldn't change a thing. I truly believe everything that we go through and don't go through is by design. There is a master plan and purpose for our lives. Now, how we navigate, move through, and handle this plan and purpose is the challenge that we are faced with. Every lesson given to us comes with a great responsibility to grow, learn, and share. We can choose to get stronger, better, and wiser. Or we can choose to lie down, cry, and stay in a state of depression. At the peak of your trauma is when your resilience factor must kick in. I've had many setbacks in life that have left me depressed, anguished, and disappointed, but through them all I've been resilient. Resiliency is a gift. A gift that most humans posses but don't understand. It is the ability to bounce back from heartache, sadness, and losses even while suffering.

CHAPTER 2

Resilience Is Your Superpower

Grow through the things you go through.
Growing through the things you go through is one part of our human experience. Not only are we flawed individuals, but our journey will be flawed. Growth is inevitable. For me, I had to learn that through my flaws and through my trials and tribulations I was going to have to depend on myself more than I anticipated. With this understanding, I found that growth is a mindset, and we can shift and change our mindset throughout our lives to better improve our chances of experiencing joy. There comes a time in life when you have to admit you are powerless. Powerless in the face of tragedy and trauma. We are all faced with trauma and tragedy. No one is exempt. I have faced my share of traumas throughout my life, and through them all I have tried to grow.

Whether it was battling breast cancer or losing a baby, I tried my best to focus on growth as a person, learn as much as I could as a decent human being, and share my story so others could heal. I can recall after losing my baby people would say to me, "Wow, you are doing so well, I don't know how you are making it." What they didn't see or know was that I was depressed.

Losing a baby was difficult. It hurt me to my core. I would cry every day for a year. I literally cried every day for a year. What kept me going was the work I was doing as an educator, an entertainment agent, and working out. I poured myself into things to escape the pain of dealing and coping. Some people may say that is not a great way to grieve a loss, but I felt like it made me stronger. Now, don't get me wrong, I was in cognitive behavioral therapy for over a year, but having other outlets built a foundation for me. This foundation created my resilience factor.

People truly underestimate the power of resilience. Resilience is your ability to recover quickly from tragedy. Resilience is the method and mode you use to bounce back. Bouncing back is what we do when we face disappointment, despair, defeat, and failure. Instead of wallowing in our hopelessness or letting things keep us down, we get back up and continue on our journey. Demonstrating resilience doesn't necessarily mean that you have not suffered. It also doesn't mean you have not experienced emotional pain, trauma, or sadness.

The road to resilience is often paved with emotional stress and anxiety. My goal was never to recover quickly. My goal was and always will be to get through challenges with the least amount of impact to my mind, body, and spirit. My resilience came naturally to me. In the moment, you think you don't have what it takes to make it through. Over time, I began to understand that the death of my daughter wasn't the death of me and that I had more life to live. I found myself trying to make sense of the tragedy. I knew I wanted to be a voice for women who had suffered pregnancy loss.

I knew I wanted the suffering to stop. I wanted to be the face of stillborn babies. I wanted to bring light to the darkness in a respectful way. This was a part of my healing process. I thought standing up as an advocate would help me. I tried to do this on many occasions, but the music business got in the way. It tested me daily.

Your tests are often your testimony. One of my biggest tests came with a diagnosis of Stage 1 breast cancer. This test was unlike any other that I've faced in my life. I mean I've had bad relationships, bad breakups, financial disappointments, and setbacks in school. I lost a baby and so much more, but getting a diagnosis of breast cancer really shifted my perspective to think, wow, life is truly short, and things can come at you abruptly. I've found that understanding the setbacks and tests you encounter in life turn into your testimony. I didn't understand this concept when I was younger. It was through getting older and wiser and suffering through a stillbirth and battling breast cancer that made me realize that we are tested, tried, and taken through the fire in life. It's how you turn these tests into your testimony that demonstrates your resilience.

I've learned that there are two types of pain in this world: pain that damages you and pain that transforms you. Oftentimes, society does not consider your suffering or pain as valid and will invalidate it most of the time. This was a tough pill to swallow and learn. You know the saying "Life goes on"? Well, for me it rang true. I found myself lying in bed crying, suffering, and feeling like crap, then I would turn on the television or look on social media, and it seemed as if life was moving. However, I was stuck. I couldn't grasp this reality. It took me weeks, even months to realize that just because you go through something truly bad in your life it doesn't mean others must stop, drop, and roll over, too. It doesn't mean that everyone around you should be in bed crying, suffering, and feeling like crap. Society does not necessarily have to validate your suffering or pain. It's not a societal problem. It's yours.

So, the moment you understand that society will invalidate your pain or step on your pain or ignore your pain, then you become free to heal. You become ready and open to embrace your process. It's nothing personal, but people don't have to care about your issues. This is why there are psychologists, therapists, and social workers. It is their job to care. They go to school to prepare themselves to care about other peoples' problems. I had to stop thinking everyone should be sad, should care, or even be concerned. This was my reality. I had to deal with it. Grasping this concept helped me grow and further strengthened my ability to bounce back and become resilient.

Resilience is your superpower. Resilience will save you from yourself. We should all seek to pursue the power of resilience with the possibility of failing and achieving the mindset of positivity. Being resilient doesn't guarantee a clean transition through life's obstacles. We will definitely encounter egregious situations that continue to challenge and bring out our negativity. Stay positive as much as you can but know that the negative thoughts and statements are perfectly normal during your pursuit of finding your resilience factor. Don't allow yourself to remain in the negativity. You see, that is the key to being resilient. Having moments and fighting through them. Remain hopeful and not hopeless. You have to keep fighting for mental clarity and stability. It's hard, but you can do it. Resilience is defined by how well you bounce back from trouble, setbacks, or challenges. Mental toughness says a lot about character. As women, we are born resilient. It's not until we are tested that we realize we have strength beyond measure.

Find triumph out of trials. Build something, create something, or start a new business venture or project. Keeping busy is the most important thing you can do after dealing with tragedy. Trust me, I know this firsthand. The only way to come out of the depths of despair is to turn your trials into triumph, your devastation into preservation. Nobody truly understands your pain unless they've gone through it. So don't expect others to "get it" because they won't. Your journey is your journey. Your family and friends are there for support (assistance) and comfort (reassurance) not answers (resolution). There is a big difference between support, comfort, and answers.

The journal at the end of this book will help you find your resilience factor. It was uniquely made and designed just for you, the reader. The exercises are designed to help you grow through what you go through and ultimately find your own resilience factor. Along with the exercises in the journal, I've developed some important lessons called Resilient Moments throughout the book that will help you build resilience.

Resilient Moments

Helpful Tips for Building Resilience

1. Avoid seeing crises as undefeatable problems.
2. Accept that change is a part of living.
3. Seek therapy early.
4. Look for opportunities for self-discovery.
5. Nurture a positive view of yourself.
6. Keep things in perspective.
7. Take care of yourself before you take care of others.
8. Find a support system.

Never be afraid to fall apart. That may sound strange, but it's real. Everyone has a breaking point. A breakdown or hitting rock bottom is your lowest point and the most vulnerable time. It also offers the opportunity to change your situation around and have it become your greatest moment. I often ask myself: *What is my rock bottom? How will I know when I've hit my rock bottom? Do you have to hit your rock bottom before you start to heal?*

Falling apart, losing it, or hitting your rock bottom for many people is part of the process. They all present an opportunity for you to rebuild yourself to be stronger and more resilient. It looks different for us all. It's an opportunity for you to transform into the person you've always wanted to be or need to be. It's extremely rare that you will find a person who has it all together and never hits a low point in life. I have had to question myself many times. *Is this my rock bottom?* is something I would ask myself after every trauma or crisis in my life. Although it may seem painful to us to break down or hit our lowest point, we have no choice but to face each one brutally, honestly, and painfully. You may think I'm crazy for saying this, but I would live this journey and do everything the same way all over again because of the incredible insight and realization that I gained. I was able to grow in my darkest hours and trust life more.

Resilient Moments

Dealing with Your Rock Bottom

1. Practice self-compassion.
2. Seek therapy.
3. Turn your pain into power.
4. See the good in yourself.
5. Take time to reflect.
6. Find a creative outlet.
7. Listen to music as often as you can.
8. Find water to look at or be by (water is healing).}

At some point in all of our lives, we are forced to deal and heal—deal with our traumas and then heal them. You can't control things that are beyond your control, but you can navigate through the pain, problems, and despair with dignity. Understanding that you have the tools within you to do this is critical to your growth as a human being. Live in the moment. Be present in your pain. Own it. Accept it and move through it. The reason I wanted to have a chapter on resilience is because I think it sets the stage for the rest of the book. I truly believe that I am resilient. I believe that I am strong. I believe that I have grown. I believe that I have recovered in many areas of my life. However, resilience is ongoing; you don't just go through something and then know how to deal with it and you're healed. You are constantly forced on a day-to-day basis to be resilient, and this I know to be true. So what I want you to take away from this chapter is what resilience is, what it looks like for me. You may even feel that some of this resonates with you, but I want you to take away one thing from this chapter. You have the ability to overcome and bounce back from anything that life throws at you. You have supernatural abilities and strength. Resilience is your superpower.

CHAPTER 3

You Can't Put a Band-Aid on a Bullet Wound

Sometimes you win, sometimes you learn.
Throughout my life, I've lost many things. Many of these losses would have broken the average person. I've been divorced, which means I've been married. I've been in toxic relationships, contemptuous breakups, and every boyfriend I've ever had has cheated on me. I've lost business deals, and over time I started to think, *Wow, I keep losing things.* As I got older and started to really live life, some of those losses mean nothing to me when I look back on them. But many of those losses were tough lessons for me. Sometimes our losses are designed to create gains. Not everything you lose is a loss. When we lose anything, it hurts. However, what we have to remember is that sometimes our losses are designed to create gains. This means sometimes when we lose something such as a relationship, car, friends, or money, God sets us up to get it back and even more later on. Or we learn a lesson from the loss that pushes us even further in life. We gain experience. We gain understanding. We gain mental toughness. Not everything you lose is a loss, because if there was a lesson from that loss it is ultimately a gain.

One of the biggest lessons that I've learned is that you cannot worry about things you've lost because they're gone. Once they're gone, they're not yours to worry about anymore. This doesn't mean you forget the memories or moments associated with these losses and situations. It means that you can't continue to live a life ruminating over people, places, and things that you have lost, as painful as it may be. When worrying ends, faith begins. Faith is another part of your resilience factor. I had to rely on my faith many times. I had to rely on myself, and I've had to rely on the strength within me to know that I can get through losses, just as I have embraced any other challenge along my journey. It wasn't until I lost a baby that my eyes were opened to what loss truly represented to me as a woman and human being. This is an important concept for everyone to understand. Losing anything close to our hearts hurts. But the loss of a human life devastates us more because there is also a loss of control that we experience simultaneously.

I wrote this book not to put a whole list of my losses and complaints in one place. I wrote this book because I really feel like people have to garner a deeper understanding of their journey through their losses, gains, ups, and downs. A big part of our journey is losing things, losing people, and sometimes losing in life. Those are just facts. While reading this chapter, I want you to face your losses and understand that they are lessons. These losses are not something to be looked at as "okay, get over it" and move on. That is not my intention. It's okay to grieve a loss, it's okay to mourn the death of a family member or friend, and it's also okay to be sad about losing a job or breaking up with a boyfriend. What's not okay is staying stuck in the depths of that loss. Your perspective has to change, and you have to focus on healing and repairing your mind and spirit. Healing doesn't replace the fact that damage and grief existed. Healing means that the damage and grief don't control our lives any longer.

I had to sit back when I hit my forties and look at my life, because in your twenties and thirties every bad thing seems like such a devastation. You view life's uncertainty and challenges with a very narrow lens. You rarely see the big picture. You are not truly equipped with all of the tools you need to get over a terrible event or triumph and overcome setbacks for the most part. I truly believe when you get in your forties there is a deeper perspective and understanding that you have about life because you've lived, loved, and lost. I was always an upbeat person. I have a big heart. I'm a giver and so, for me, I always wanted to fix and help other people through their losses or setbacks. But when I noticed that, I would look around, and there was no one there to help me through some of my deepest and darkest periods. I realized you have to help yourself. I had to learn to be resilient. I had to face every loss on my own, to a certain degree, either because I was afraid to speak up or people just didn't know I was in pain. Now don't get me wrong, I had a family that supported me. I had friends and boyfriends who were a part of my support system. However, at the end of the day they can't fix you, they can't bring back the baby, they can't take away the breast cancer, and they definitely can't bring back a broken relationship. I had to be stronger. I realize that everyone thought I was strong and had it all going on. Sometimes when you are a giver and you're always trying to help, fix, and build others up, people will assume you are okay. I learned to fight, and I learned to fight on my own most of the time. Fighting through the highs and lows is the most exhausting process ever, but I did it. Sometimes you win, sometimes you lose, and every time you learn. In all you do, find the lesson and learn from it.

I have to tell a story here because I feel like I need to be vulnerable to be believable. When I was in college, I was dating a guy that I was madly in love with, but I don't think he was madly in love with me. I found out he was cheating on me with someone I knew, and I fought so hard to keep this relationship going even though I knew he was cheating on me. I forgave him and then I took him back and later on I ended up marrying him, which in turn led to a divorce later on. Looking back at that experience I feel like once I found out that he was cheating on me with a friend of mine, actually a sorority sister, I should have just let that go. But I was so focused on trying to make it work and trying to not suffer a loss that I lost myself. Or I was trying not to look stupid in front of people, so I forced it to work. Even when this person was not my soulmate and we really had nothing in common. We had nothing in common! This person should not have been my first husband. So, that takes me back to my earlier point that losses are lessons, and I can look back and be mad or learn the lesson. I moved on from that relationship. Going forward in life, I noticed this happened to me a lot, especially in my twenties. I encountered more losses of boyfriends, bad breakups, and relationships because I didn't heal properly from past experiences. I started to see patterns of getting in relationships where the person would cheat on me and I would stay because I didn't want to suffer a loss, and then the relationship ultimately ended. I found myself constantly trying to bounce back or recover. I didn't learn my lesson right away. However, I was able to recover more quickly from bad breakups because those were familiar situations for me. I was able to heal from breakups because I knew the formula. I had the tools to survive and move on. Even today, I still struggle with when to let go, when to move forward, and I think that's a big part of understanding how to recover from relationship losses.

Losing a baby changed me. I was pregnant and found out in the middle of the semester. As a professor teaching college, I was forced to live my life in front of hundreds of people. Everyone on campus knew I was pregnant, so losing the baby had an even deeper and darker effect on me because it was in front of the world. After losing the baby, I can recall when I returned from being out on disability getting in the elevator and running into one of my former students. They asked me, "Professor, how is the baby?" I just remembered I wanted to shrink into a hole and never return. That was a painful moment. I said, "Oh, the baby passed away" with a stoic look on my face. They apologized profusely, but it wasn't their fault. They did not know. I encountered that scenario about a dozen more times. I eventually started hiding and taking the stairs to avoid large crowds. Looking back, that was the right thing to do.

Resilient Moments

Coping Strategies for Loss

1. Realize you are in an exclusive club of mothers who have babies born into heaven.
2. You have to demand respect, privacy, and your right to heal, grieve, and be left alone.
3. Trust your instinct and go to the doctor as often as you feel.
4. Physical therapy is important if you suffer any kind of injury from the delivery or pregnancy.
5. Take care of your mind, body, and soul.
6. Feed your spirit with as much positive material as you can.
7. Don't blame yourself.
8. Don't rush the process.
9. Watch comedies. You will need to laugh at some point. The smiles are not as often as the cries.
10. Keeping busy is the most important thing you can do after having a stillbirth or miscarriage.
11. Get an autopsy. It will save you grief later on. Have a specialist read the autopsy.
12. Go to therapy.
13. Develop a response to "Did you have the baby?" or "What happened?" You have the right to ignore it, move on, or say exactly how you feel.
14. Take a vacation. Get away.
15. Understand that kick counts are important.
16. Get tested, treated, and diagnosed. I would recommend figuring out what happened before getting pregnant again.

Losing a baby and being diagnosed with cancer were not familiar situations for me, so the recovery time was more difficult, harder, and unique. I needed more time to heal from both of these situations. When you are fighting through breast cancer, you are exhausted. You are constantly working out and eating right, having radiation, getting second opinions, and traveling back and forth to doctors' appointments. This loss I describe as a loss of control. It was something that I was not prepared for. It wasn't a part of my family history. So, I describe this loss as a loss of control over my health and life at that time.

I think people tend to lump all of their setbacks or issues in one box. That is not healthy to do. They are all different. Suffering from a stillbirth, breast cancer, and a bad breakup are all viewed from a different lens, in my opinion. Losing a baby was a massive and more significant trauma than failing in relationships. It's very difficult to overcome this type of pain and loss. I know a lot of women who have not healed from this type of loss. It is hard to bounce back and be resilient in the face of a miscarriage or stillbirth. Losing a baby is one of those traumas that require extensive amounts of therapy, support groups, and cognitive behavioral therapy. I was in therapy for over a year after losing my baby. I had sessions once per week for about sixty weeks. They were necessary. My therapist diagnosed me with PTSD. There were constant guilt breakdowns and flashbacks during the healing process. It's a pain I don't wish on anyone. It is a trauma that creates extreme anxiety and constant second-guessing. This was a tough situation to heal from. But with God, faith, and tapping into my resilience factor, I did it.

Measuring your traumas can be therapeutic because each tragedy or occurrence is special. It's really how you process each event, deal with it, and heal from it. I like to view the losses we encounter as cuts or wounds to our body that must be healed first before we can continue on our journey in happiness. As you encounter setbacks and losses, don't put a Band-Aid on it. Let the wound heal and seek therapy early and often. As a mentor and business coach, I tell my clients all the time to write it down and that journaling can be therapeutic. That's what I focused on with my healing process. I went to therapy and started to write. I started to pour myself into my health and wellness, to get my body right and my mind right, and I also started to dig deeper into my business and develop my personal brand.

I decided to write this chapter and call it "You Can't Put a Band-Aid on a Bullet Wound" because I feel like, oftentimes, when we lose things or bad things in life happen to us that may not be ideal or the plan we had in our minds, we don't fully heal. We have to learn to protect ourselves from emotional wounds. The takeaway from this chapter is that you can't put a Band-Aid on a bullet wound, and you must address the hurt and pain directly. You must diagnose each wound individually. Don't cover it up. I know it is hard to address your wounds and realize that you have to give up control and face the agony. Healing is worth it. Your resilient mindset can heal your wounds.

CHAPTER 4

Turning Into Wonder Woman

G *ood health can give you superhuman powers.* Throughout my life, especially early on, I struggled with my weight and seeing my health as wealth. I constantly felt like I was either too big or too skinny, but I never put in the time to figure out what health meant to me rather than what others saw of me. I have yo-yo dieted most of my life. There was a love-hate relationship with food. I never really understood the purpose of food until I got older. Food was viewed as comfort. It was a way to hide some of the pain I endured as a young child. I ate as a means of masking certain things I was depressed about. As a child, I was sheltered and shy in the school system. I was the middle child at home, so I think that gave me a unique experience—too young for my older sister and too old for my younger sister. I believe, looking back, I ate certain things out of boredom. I loved apple pies, cakes, and sweets. All of these items barely get touched now.

Of course, like most black families, I grew up on the soul food diet. Cornbread, fried chicken, and macaroni and cheese were items my mother could throw down on! My mother was a remarkable cook. My father owned a chain of fish restaurants (Solomon's Fishery) throughout Chicago, which was where I worked for a short time as a teenager. It can feel like an ongoing battle not to indulge frequently in soul food when it's so heavily ingrained into black culture. Every major event, like birthdays, parties, holidays, and baby showers, can have all sorts of soul food brought to the table. You name it, and soul food is there at a black family function.

When I was younger, I wasn't fat. But because I wasn't very slim and I was more statuesque due to my height, my cousins would call me names. I would be called anything from names like "chinchilla" and just "fat." It left a heavy impression on me as a ten-year-old. I walked through life with little to no confidence throughout fifth, sixth, and seventh grade. The mental toll of these names and treatment from my family at such an early age set the course for how my relationship with my body would change. This created the negative view I had of myself because of the name-calling by my family. From this point in my life going forward, it was hard for me to see myself and my body in a positive light.

As a kid, I wasn't very active. I did go outside, playing like most kids did back then. Unlike other kids at that time, I had interests elsewhere that didn't involve sports. There were many times that I saw women who looked like actual superheroes, in life and on television. They had the confidence and beauty that was regarded as "natural beauty." That energy radiated from them. They were beating the odds and taking the reins of their happiness, health, and life. Wonder

Woman was a popular television figure I admired. She represented strength and boldness, but because of my life at home and in school, I never truly felt like I could become a wonder woman of my own.

I did try out for girls' basketball in the eighth grade. I knew nothing about basketball and how to play! I tried out just to try and be a bit more active, but I didn't make the team. I remember looking at all the other girls, especially those who were invested in the sport, and I felt like the oddball. I was just there because I was tall. I was in no shape for playing basketball, but my gym teacher recommended it. They did put me in the position as the team manager, which feels fitting because of where I am today as an entertainment manager.

The summer of my seventh grade, I was put on a diet because I had gained weight. As a preteen this can be a jarring time. Between puberty, hormones, and just transitioning from being a young kid to a teen, it can be a lot. I was already getting teased about my weight amongst family, and it was a rough time being seen as overweight in school as well. So when I gained thirty pounds, a doctor decided that I needed to go on a diet. It made things worse looking at this doctor, as he was overweight. It was ridiculous being told by an overweight doctor that I was also overweight. This gave me an early insight into the healthcare system and how it treats people. Looking back at it now, it was the dumbest diet ever! My diet consisted of egg whites, crackers, tuna, and fruit. My calorie intake every day had to total up to 600 or 700 calories, but at that moment in my life as a twelve-year-old, there was no arguing with my family or the doctor. And there was no one telling me or supporting me enough to make sure it wasn't a mentally exhausting experience for a twelve-year-old. My family wasn't giving me that support. I remember how often I would see my mother cooking soul food and foods that weren't a part of my strict diet. I was exhausted from being bullied and having my self-esteem attacked, and a deep depression grew because of it. I needed to be uplifted, given confidence, and taught many more lessons to be like the wonder woman I watched on television.

In high school and college I was overweight. I was a size fourteen, but now we know that the average woman is a size fourteen. But at the age of fourteen, this wasn't a good size to be. I was involved in clubs, but I wasn't very physically active. I loved to dress up and make clothes. My mother bought me a sewing machine, and I would design, sketch, and sew. I developed an interest in making garments for myself and my younger sister, Syleena. By making my own clothes, I didn't have to adhere to any size constraints. I could be me and be free. However, high school was boring for me, and it just wasn't fun. I didn't get involved in sports or many other extracurricular activities because of how bored I was. I was a nerd; I even carried a briefcase. I took extra classes to just be done with high school sooner.

My weight fluctuated in college. I went to Southern Illinois University in the fall of 1990. In college, you are already low on funds, so eating right feels like a challenge. When I lost a lot of weight during this time in college, my junior year, it got to the point where my family even looked at me and said, "You look sickly!"

This alone made me think: *Do you want me to be fat or skinny? Which one is it?* I felt like I had to live up to these constant expectations of how I should look. College is a stressful time for anyone. Stress can cause many people to experience the much-talked-about freshman fifteen or lose a lot of weight. It's always a funny joke and stereotype to make about college freshmen, but no one talks about the amounts of stress that can come from essentially starting a new life in this major transition from high school to college. I was in a new environment, living with people that were so different from what I was used to and experiencing new things. So while it was an exciting time, it was just like any life-changing experience with its own ups and downs. It was overwhelming in the beginning. I lived with roommates, and while we did our own grocery shopping and cooking, we did indulge in fast food from time to time.

I graduated from college with a bachelor's in economics. I moved down to Tampa, Florida, for grad school. I lived with my boyfriend at the time and his cousins and found myself juggling work and my master's degree. I was able to keep my weight fairly consistent, but I still didn't have my best body. I was lacking the knowledge of how to eat right. Four months later, my boyfriend and I got a place of our own. I wasn't happy despite accomplishing so much. I worked in investments and got my master's degree, but eventually I had to leave four years later to come back to Chicago. It wasn't a happy time in my life. In my twenties and thirties, my understanding of health and wellness was poor. I think that once you understand health, wellness, and fitness, you get an advantage in fighting through traumatic events. This wasn't always the case, but it can be said that your physical health can impact your mental health. Because I didn't have a grasp on my health and wellness, it did a lot of damage to my body.

I was in therapy for a year and a half after losing the baby. I was drinking every day for about two weeks. This was something I knew I couldn't sustain. I saw myself wallowing in a deep and dark place. My health was not important to me at that time. I was depressed and at risk of letting myself go. I gained a lot of weight. It was a dark place that I didn't see myself getting out of. My doctor put me on Xanax, but after getting on it I realized that it wasn't for me. I wasn't going to die. I didn't want to go the route of self- medicating. While medication works for some, I just didn't enjoy doctors trying to drug me up! I took them about eight to ten times and felt ridiculous and drowsy. I don't know how people get hooked on drugs. Prescription pills only mask the pain. I needed to face my issues head-on without the influence of anxiety or pain medication. For me, being resilient meant getting my health and wellness back in order without Xanax.

I started to work with a physical therapist, Dr. Ivan Hernandez, who is also a fitness advocate and later became one of my clients. I originally began seeing him because I was experiencing nerve pain from the stillbirth that gave me tremendous pain in my legs. While I think that it was from the epidural I received during labor, they ultimately told me the cause of the pain was meralgia paresthetica, a condition that occurs from the pressure of giving birth and going through such intense labor. I was going to therapy three times per week and trying to climb my way out of a dark place mentally and physically. Dr. Ivan pushed me into the weight-loss challenge. When I was pregnant, I gained over fifty pounds. Dr. Ivan kept insisting I participate. I lost twenty-four pounds in six weeks. I won the entire challenge. I was so dedicated and motivated. I became relentless. There were fifty people signed up for the challenge. I beat out all fifty people, and it gave me a drive I never knew I had in me. My competitive spirit was alive. I was feeling better than I had in a very long time. This was my newfound passion and obsession.

Winning the contest taught me how to eat better, about inflammation, and about proper exercising. I learned just how much inflammation is the cause of disease. I lost seventy pounds, going from 240 to 170. I found myself getting into showcases and deadlifting and powerlifting, and even helping others focus on their weight. I felt unstoppable. I was becoming my own wonder woman and even surrounding myself with other wonder women who also wanted to be the best versions of themselves. I wanted to continue to uplift and motivate not only others around me but keep reminding myself that I was in control of my destiny. I was pushing myself and using deadlifting as the driving force in my life to remember that if there's a will, there's a way. I was beating the odds, transforming into a better me. But this transformation felt like it came to an abrupt halt when I felt a lump on my breast in August of 2019.

I visited my gynecologist the next day. She thought it was weird. She scheduled me for an ultrasound, and they thought it was weird. I got scheduled for a biopsy, and they thought it was weird. The next day, I got news that made my entire life flash before my eyes. My diagnosis of Stage 1 breast cancer shook me to the core. I immediately went into panic mode. It was completely different from my stillbirth journey. This was now my life on the line. In my mind, I'm healthy! No one in my family had breast cancer. I was researching and finding so many articles that showed me nothing but death sentences. It felt like hope was nowhere to be found when I needed it. There was no light at the end of the tunnel I could see.

It was an estrogen-based ERPR-positive breast cancer. ERPR-positive, also known as hormone receptor-positive, means all the estrogen and progesterone I was producing was being eaten by the cancer cells and making them grow even more. This type of breast cancer is the most common, as it makes up about 70 to 80 percent of all breast cancer cases. It was a terrifying moment in my life to find out about this diagnosis. I was feeling like I was at my healthiest and most knowledgeable about the ins and outs of my body and wellness to only get one of the most shocking diagnoses of my life. It changed how I looked at my health and life. It almost made me feel like I couldn't be that wonder woman I set out to be. I was feeling defeated, another battle that was taking its toll on me.

I had to get a lumpectomy. Removing the lump of breast tissue that was the source of so much fear and confusion was my main concern, but any major surgery is nerve-wracking. I had support from my family and boyfriend. But this surgery meant so much more for my future, my life, and most importantly my health. I was ecstatic when surgery was over. It was out of me! I was filled with hope again. I could move on with my life and start fighting for my body.

The next step was even more crucial to ensuring that the cancer didn't come back. I went through twenty rounds of radiation in four weeks. It was like living through hell. Despite pushing through it, I fought to manage all of my daily life while undertaking radiation, an experience that I will never forget. I had to still work and go about my life, going to speaking engagements and traveling during the weekend. The pain after weeks of radiation was exhausting. I was fatigued, experiencing memory loss, and my breast turned black-looking, almost burnt. I would come home and sleep for hours. I will be honest, radiation sleep was some of the best sleep of my life. It knocked me out!

Radiation taught me a lot though. I would see so many people who had friends and family members with them in radiation, while I was alone every treatment. Though I did have people there by my side in doctor's visits, it made me think about how often I put others before myself. Now with my breast cancer diagnosis, I learned to put myself first because it was a necessity. I had to put my life into perspective. The priority was my health. I couldn't be the wonder woman I needed myself to be if I didn't make me and my health the utmost priority. I was trying to still work out and eat right, but I couldn't be as active as before. I remember thinking through so much of this, *What's the lesson here, God?* Looking at the stories of women just like me gave me strength and the courage to power through every single chapter of my breast cancer journey. So many different women with different lives who had to make the same sacrifices or go through similar pains like me to beat breast cancer. The breast cancer diagnosis was a changing point for me, showing me that I could bounce back from anything. I was a wonder woman, beating the odds stacked against me.

Exercise and nutrition became an obsession. Over the years, I learned a lot about my body and what it responds to as it relates to exercise. I have found that HIIT routines, powerlifting, and circuit training are the most effective ways for me to lose weight and stay in shape. Working with my client and physical therapist Dr. Ivan Hernandez taught me a lot about the human body and its ability to adapt and transform.

After losing the baby, exercise became part of my daily regimen. It helped me to survive. It became the catalyst I needed to fight depression. Exercise is also an activity that improves your mental health. It is one of the most important things you can do to change your life. Exercise helps people lose weight and decreases a person's risk of developing certain diseases, including obesity, type 2 diabetes, and high blood pressure.

Exercising frequently also helps a person age well. As a woman of color in her forties, I began to transition my thinking from surviving to thriving. A lot of black families don't teach us how to eat correctly. We get so stuck on surviving that we don't give our bodies the chance to thrive and be healthy. Getting out of that mindset enabled me to see the benefits of treating my body with love. There are benefits of exercise that have helped me push through and bounce back over and over again. I can't stress enough the power of a healthy body.

Resilient Moments

The Benefits of Exercise

1. Exercise controls weight.
2. Exercise combats health conditions and diseases.
3. Exercise improves mood.
4. Exercise boosts energy.
5. Exercise promotes better sleep.

If you want to feel better, improve your energy capacity, and build strength, exercise is the primary way to do this. My discovery about exercise was pretty late in life. I don't care what stage of life you are in, you have to start an exercise program. You will feel better. I wish I was more active as a young child. I wish I had been more focused on sports. Although I wasn't fortunate to build a strong physical fitness background at an early age, I believe learning about fitness and wellness in my thirties and becoming more educated about it in my forties has allowed me to reach fitness goals at various levels. And I loved that because you can start exercising and changing your life at any point! You are never too old. I have witnessed women in their sixties and seventies powerlifting and bodybuilding, more cases of being a wonder woman at any age. Inspiration knows no age limit. I used the motivation and confidence gained later in life to become the wonder woman I needed in my youth.

Powerlifting spoke to my heart in a way that other exercises didn't. I built a fondness for powerlifting after Dr. Ivan encouraged me to start increasing my deadlift weight. I started building my strength, and that became an addiction for me. Every week my deadlift numbers would rise. Starting out at a 135-pound lift and progressing to 240 pounds became an awesome accomplishment for me. It was exhilarating! It gave me an unexpected rush that no other exercises were giving me. I want people to explore what makes them their own wonder woman. For me it was powerlifting. Powerlifting made me resilient.

Physical strength gave me inner strength. I was hitting my stride and becoming an inspiration for others to find theirs too. I would have never thought I would be in my forties lifting heavy weights, screaming at the deadlift bar, getting my back slapped, and powerlifting, when at the age of twelve I was put on a diet and told I was overweight. For me, this was a full-circle moment in my life. I have found that powerlifting has provided me many benefits that I continue to share with others.

Resilient Moments

The Benefits of Powerlifting

1. Fat Loss
2. Improved Strength
3. Better Skeletal Health
4. Increase in Athletic Ability

5. Increase in Muscle Mass and Improvement in Posture
6. Powerlifting Slows the Aging Process

With my love for exercising and powerlifting, I realized I had to make changes to what I consumed. I researched every nutritional topic there was until I found things that made sense for my lifestyle. Let's be clear, I love food! But you can't let food ruin your life. When I first started my wellness journey in 2014, I learned about the Whole30 Diet. This is a diet based on eating all whole foods from the earth and eliminating things out of your diet, like sugar, alcohol, grains, legumes, soy, and dairy. It was practical, easy, and made perfect sense for me. Humans have become so engulfed with processed foods that we have forgotten about the basics: fruits, vegetables, and wild-caught fish. This diet was essential in my wellness journey and in giving me the energy and confidence I needed for so many years. I started to learn more about the body and inflammation and how food played a role in that. I also started to do intermittent fasting, where I would eat for a certain period of time and then fast afterward for a period of time. During the fasting periods, you eat either very little or nothing at all. My window of eating was from 12 p.m. to 8 p.m.

With all of these learned principles, the most important thing I have discovered about turning into a wonder woman was that you have to first love yourself the way you are. Wonder Woman was confident, even in her roughest of moments. She was described as a warrior princess of the Amazon. Confidence is a feeling of self-assurance arising from one's appreciation of one's own abilities or qualities.

Confidence is the key to great health and resilience. It is a daily battle, but I am working toward becoming more and more confident in myself, my abilities, and the way I deal with other people. Confidence creates the environment to become resilient.

The more confident you are the more you begin to fight for your rights as it relates to your health and the healthcare system. I learned a lot going through a stillbirth, breast cancer, and weight loss. I learned that I had to be the boss of my recovery. I learned that I had to question the doctors, get second opinions, and fight insurance companies any chance I got. Doctors don't really tell you everything you need to know. That's not their job. Our healthcare system has become so convoluted and corrupt that you literally have to verify, check, and research everything told to you. The cost of maintaining good health is also outrageous. During my journey, I have found that great habits can lead to lower medical costs. Some things are not preventable, but the only way to win this battle of great health is to truly do the best you can from a prevention perspective. My weight loss journey was designed by science and created so that I could implement most of it on a daily basis. That is the key to sticking to a plan and routine. It must be simple, easy, and backed by science.

Resilient Moments

My Weight Loss Journey
1. Paleo-based Diet and Intermittent Fasting
2. HIIT (High-Intensity Interval Training)

3. Powerlifting/Weight Training
4. Six to Eight Hours of Sleep
5. Meditation and Stress Reduction
6. Discipline and Consistency

As I look back on my journey with health and wellness and the role it has played in my resilience factor, I am truly grateful for the losses, gains, and experiences that I have encountered. From not being very active as a child to deadlifting 240 pounds and losing seventy pounds, I found my inner strength and ability. I became my very own Wonder Woman.

CHAPTER 5
The Hero's Journey

You are always the hero in your story.

A hero can be defined as a person who is admired or idealized for courage, outstanding achievements, or noble qualities. The hero's journey is a classic story structure that was coined by Joseph Campbell in 1949. This concept is used in many of the movies that we've watched and admired over the years. It refers to a wide-ranging category of tales in which a character ventures out to get what they need; they come into contact with trials and conflict and then ultimately triumph over adversity. I love this concept. It's the perfect analogy to apply to your life. The concept of the hero's journey is simple, and we can apply it to our own lives. This classic storyline structure helps us to understand and to overcome most of the ups and downs of this journey. Just think about your favorite movie. From movies like *Rocky* to *The Lion King* and *Black Panther*, each of them had a hero who faced a difficult and devastating conflict, or struggled, and ultimately became victorious in the end and beat adversity.

You are the hero of your own life story. Wherever you stand in your hero's journey, I hope this chapter helps you to realize that you are a hero. There will always be trying times and difficult moments that we are forced to deal with. It is in these times that we must dig deep within ourselves and purposefully seek out solutions and that inner ability to fight. The hero's journey is not always pretty. It is paved with despair, destruction, and disbelief. There will be plenty of times where you want to give up during your journey. I hope this chapter also forces you to look at your circumstances and to jump over your shadow by taking leaps toward your ultimate victory. Throughout your journey, you will be faced with temptation to give up, but in every circumstance there needs to be a plan of action and tools to help you get through to win over this crisis and to come back as a changed and transformed person.

We also have to study the hero's journey from the viewpoint of losing in the end. In reality, the endings of most of our stories aren't always pretty. The victory looks different for each person. How you go through it truly determines your heroism. I feel there are two ways to look at the hero's journey. One ending focuses on winning a total victory over whatever obstacle you faced. The other ending is the impact you made on the people around you and how you fought through your journey. So, for example, someone may battle breast cancer but ultimately succumb to the disease. Would we say they weren't victorious? Would we say that their journey ended in failure? How would we categorize this particular hero's journey? I feel like the encounters you face should always be measured by the heroic feats that you have overcome. It's not about the end; it's about the path we took to get there. At the end of the day, circumstances are always built for us to win. We just have to believe.

Throughout my life, I've had several journeys where I was the hero in each. My latest test was my battle with breast cancer. I didn't feel like a hero in the beginning, and I didn't feel that I could overcome it either. This journey started the day I found the lump. The infamous lump in my left breast. I was in shock and disbelief. I called my gynecologist immediately to set up an appointment for her to examine it. She thought it was strange, and so she had me go and get an ultrasound. The doctor who did my ultrasound thought it looked strange on the screen, and it was not conclusive if it was something to be worried about, so she ordered a biopsy. Once they told me I needed a biopsy, that is when I began to worry. I will never forget that the biopsy took place on a Wednesday, and I got the results back on that Thursday. She called and she said your results came back and you have Stage 1 breast cancer. I immediately started to cry. I just knew it was the end for me. In all seriousness, I was freaked out. Just look at my life. I've been working out. I had just lost seventy pounds. I thought I was this pillar of health, and to be told that my breast cancer was ER, which is estrogen, and PR, which is progesterone positive, was shocking. That meant I had a hormonal imbalance, and the estrogen was feeding the cancer. The lump was about the size of a strawberry, but once they took it out it was a little bigger than they expected. It could have been reclassified as Stage 2, but my doctor said it was irrelevant because the tumor was out.

I cried for hours and hours. I called my boyfriend first, then my sisters, and finally my mother. It had to be the second worst day of my life, next to finding out my daughter didn't have a heartbeat. This journey looked like a fool. I just knew this journey was going to either make or break me.

Once I got into the realization that I had to undergo surgery, which was a lumpectomy, I immediately went into activation mode. My friend and physical therapist, Dr. Ivan, was a very big help for me. He suggested I reach out to Dr. Kasia, who immediately put me on an eating plan and supplement routine to fight the cancer. I am a strong believer in supplements and healing our bodies with natural techniques. My surgery was scheduled for three weeks from the day I found out. So you can imagine the amount of freaking out and crying and anxiety that I had just waiting for that day. But during those three weeks I was on a very strict regimen with taking supplements, praying, and working out. I was determined to beat cancer and beat it badly. I was preparing each day for the surgery. I was preparing my mind, my body, and my spirit. I knew I had overcome so many things in my life, but this one seemed different. Having Stage 1 breast cancer seemed like a death sentence when I was first told. Eventually, I was able to do a lot of research and wrap my mind around this diagnosis.

The surgery took about one hour, and I was in the hospital for about six hours total. It was outpatient surgery. I had my boyfriend there and my sister Sylette. We were in a positive mood. I couldn't imagine going through this surgery alone. I felt anxious and nervous but happy it was going to be taken out.

It's the weirdest thing in life to walk around with cancer in you. You feel hopeless. There is a part of you that feels like any day something bad could happen. I wish I could have gotten the surgery the next day, but the doctor said it didn't work like that. When I arrived at the hospital, we waited about an hour. Once I went inside to prep for the surgery, I knew this could be the beginning of the end of cancer for me. I can recall being on the hospital bed and asking a lot of questions about the surgery. My nerves were bad and got to me. Once they put the anesthesia in me, it was a wrap. I just remember waking up and telling them I dreamt about Chris Brown. It was odd but hilarious.

After the surgery I had to go into recovery of my body and my spirit in a way that I had never experienced. It's strange because I can recall a week and a half after my surgery, I was traveling for an event that my client and sister Syleena had in Chicago. I was still bandaged and in excruciating pain, but I got on that flight and I attended that event. It was a black Greek step show event that she served as a judge for and it gave me an opportunity to connect with my sorority sister and good friend, Tywanda.

Over the next two to three months, I traveled to speak to women at various conferences and went through twenty rounds of radiation. My doctors let me travel on the weekends. My radiation oncologist actually encouraged me to keep going on with my normal life. He said it would make me feel better and that I can't let the radiation stop me. This was great advice. Many people thought I was crazy, but I found the right balance. Over a period of four months, I met with my medical oncologist and radiologist from Mount Sinai Hospital in New York City. Both of them were amazing. The doctor who did my lumpectomy, Dr. Estabrook, was awesome as well. I had a great medical team.

I didn't know how tough I had to be until my first week in radiation. That pain and fatigue were debilitating. I had five sessions a week, Monday through Friday, going back and forth on the train by myself. Radiation is something I don't wish on my worst enemy. It's a fool. It's exhausting and the pain afterward is unbearable, but you get through it. The fact that I traveled and had to do speaking engagements while going through radiation made my journey even more crazy with a touch of exhilaration.

I flew to California twice. I spoke at the SoCal Women's Conference in Pasadena, California. I was a panelist for The Best Me Conference in Oakland, California. One of my fondest moments was speaking at The BOSS Network's tenth-anniversary conference in Chicago, Illinois, during October, which was breast cancer awareness month. The bonus of being at the conference was meeting Tina Knowles-Lawson, Melody Spann-Cooper, and supermodel Beverly Johnson. These were powerful women I have always admired in the entertainment and music industry. Sitting on the panel next to Beverly Johnson was an outstanding feeling. The participants in the audience were in shock when I said on stage how I was supposed to start radiation the following week. I said it so casually because at that point I was going through the motions. Afterward I could tell what I said made an impact on the women there. A lot of them came up to me to say that I was strong and a warrior and to take care of myself.

This was another reminder of my resilience factor. You don't know this is a sign of strength until you reflect about these moments you have lived and survived. It was important for me to fulfill these speaking obligations and share my story. Being around women made it easier for me to get well and push through the recovery process.

Resilient Moments

Coping Strategies for Survivors

1. Invest in a nutritionist or registered dietician.
2. Go to therapy.
3. Be informed and inquisitive every step of the process: after diagnosis and after treatment.
4. Exercise four to five times per week.
5. Be kind to yourself.
6. Do things you enjoy. Live your life to the fullest.

As I write this, I feel like this journey is ongoing. I do understand and realize that I'm a hero. I was a hero throughout each challenge and throughout my journey. It takes determination and strength to fight through and battle cancer. The road was not easy, but I had great doctors and a support system in place. What I realized was I had to take this journey alone. I began to write my thoughts down, formalize the book I had in my mind, and reflect on where I've been and where I was going.

Writing became a part of my daily activities. I would keep notes in my phone, send myself emails, and go on social media and use that platform to encourage and empower others. Writing is therapeutic.

Whether it be journaling, blogging, creating social media posts, or writing a book, I discovered that you can work through anything if you write your thoughts and fears down. Telling your story can change and save a life, especially your own.

Over the years, I have trained hundreds of people who had a desire to write a book, but never started the process. As humans, we all have a unique journey and story. Don't let that story die inside of you. Share it. Speak it. Give it to the world. You never know how your words or truth may impact the lives of other people. The more you grow, the more comfortable you become telling your story. This is also a true sign of resilience. When you can share or talk about your story to others, you know you've been healed from whatever it was that was holding you back.

The hero's journey is a perspective that can change your life for the good. Although it is used in movie scripts, it can also be used in your life. Art often imitates life. We are always going to encounter challenges, obstacles, and trauma on a regular basis. We must continually cycle through various stages in life to become our best selves and achieve our purpose. There are many ways to apply the hero's journey to your life.

Resilient Moments

Applying Your Hero's Journey

1. Realize that you are a HERO.
2. Practice self-discovery through exercises (the journal at the end of the book will help you).

3. Recognize the signs and know when you are facing a challenge.
4. Eliminate fear.
5. Leave your comfort zone.
6. Get therapy, a life coach, or a support system.
7. Rely on your experiences and draw upon your faith.
8. Face any roadblock with your truth.
9. Look at overcoming life's obstacles as a reward.
10. Continue to learn and grow through it all.

My hero's journey was plagued literally with disease and despair, but I overcame it. Now, I'm able to write about it. This is an opportunity for me to inspire someone else to fight through their cancer battle or any other battle they may face. It's also an opportunity for me to heal. I feel like I won the battle with breast cancer, but I also understand that it's an ongoing battle and I have to take care of myself. I have to eat right. I have to watch my caffeine and alcohol intake. I have to monitor my inflammation and watch the foods I eat. My diet had to change dramatically. I have to be mindful of soy. I have to be mindful of what I ingest and digest in my body and in my spirit. Stress is a killer. Reducing stress is a must for every breast cancer survivor and for people in general. It wreaks havoc on the body. I have to focus on cleansing and preparing my body because this journey to stay cancer-free will be my ultimate test.

CHAPTER 6

Leaving the Rat Race

You have full control over your destiny.
Starting a business can change your life. Entrepreneurship has always been a desire of mine. Even as a young girl I always admired businesspeople and I always looked up to those who were creators. When you start a business and are self-employed, you are your own boss and ultimately control your own destiny.

Going to college at the age of seventeen was an eye-opener for me. College did not properly prepare me to pick the right career path. As I got older, I changed majors in college several times. I had about six or seven different majors. I ended my major confusion with graduating from Southern Illinois University in Edwardsville with a Bachelor of Science in economics. I then went on to get a master's degree from a small business college in Tampa, Florida, and my doctorate in business administration. I was preparing for a world in corporate America. I had no idea my career path would shift.

Throughout my life I've worked in nonprofit organizations, for-profit corporations, small government agencies, and college systems, but I've always maintained the entrepreneurial mindset. I started working independently in 2002 as Syleena's business manager. I was kind of pushed into this role because she had fired her business manager at the time and needed someone to help with her expenses and finances. Many people at that time knew me as an educator and a corporate employee. I am still a full-time professor. I've been teaching since 2001, but they also knew me as the person who works in entertainment. I have been a manager in many roles in the music business, such as music business manager, road manager, and entertainment agent for about twenty years now, and it's been exhilarating. It's been fascinating, it's been full of highs and lows, but one thing I can say is that being an entrepreneur, as well as an educator, I've learned a lot about what's acceptable and what's not. I've learned that sometimes when we have something of our own that's a source of inspiration and through all of the things that I've gone through, all of the losses, ups and downs, I could always pull inspiration from the work that I was doing with my business.

When I lost the baby I had to go on disability and wasn't earning as much money. Entrepreneurship saved me. If I hadn't owned my own company and had another way of earning extra money, I would have been broke and filed for bankruptcy. I would have been ruined.

So, people may wonder why this chapter is here. This chapter is to encourage you to start something new as a means of bouncing back or recovering from whatever it is you're going through. You don't have to start a business, but you should start something. For me it was continuing on with my business and pouring myself into my work and new projects. It was my creative space and place to be innovative. It was also a means of additional income.

Having a business helped me grow as a person. When you have your own business and simultaneously go through some difficult situations, you get a better understanding of your character and your resiliency. There is more self-discovery, and you truly have to lean in on your faith. The reason why having a business helped me grow is because I could always count on myself. Even if the personal side of my life was falling apart or I was being challenged in other areas, I could use the professional side of my life to look at and pull hope from.

When I transitioned from the corporate world to just teaching and running my business, I felt a sense of freedom. It was me leaving the rat race. Now, I am not against anyone working in corporate America or working a nine-to-five job, but I truly believe that some of the most resilient people on earth are entrepreneurs. We are risk-takers. We are go-getters. We are innovators. And you find out who is who when your back is against the wall. You have your own business, but you're also going through personal, professional, and financial woes. You really do find out who is who and what people are made of when you study entrepreneurs, and I feel like that was part of my calling, to be an entrepreneur. I feel like it was also part of my healing process because I had something to fall back on. I did not want to let myself down, but also I wanted to keep my business thriving because I had clients. This chapter is dedicated to all of the entrepreneurs out there that also go through things and use their resiliency, however they can.

I have coached thousands of people over the past twenty-plus years. There is one thing that I can take away from coaching so many people as it relates to business or entrepreneurship and that is people are afraid to start something new. Most people are not risk-takers. They are scared to do things on their own, and I think this plays a big role in how resilient one can be. Think about it for a second. If you start a new project or start a business or just start something different, you have to face your fear of failure. You have to deal with it as you do with suffering other losses, traumas, or tragedy. You have to face your fears in the end. You have to maintain and be an active participant in the process. You can't escape your business. You have to work toward fixing anything that goes wrong. It doesn't have to be quick, but it has to be some type of recovery. You have to face your fears, you have to do self-discovery, and so that's what I love about training people and coaching is that I get them to face their fears.

After you read this chapter, I hope you want to start something new that becomes a part of your healing process, or you just get a spark of creativity. I'm not forcing you to start a business. I'm not forcing you to become an entrepreneur, but what I am trying to instill in you is that having something to fall back on or to invest your time and energy into can be a part of your healing or a new chapter in life. Because when you look at the rat race, it is tough, and the entrepreneur race is even tougher. However, I feel good about having my own story about pouring myself into this business and how it made me feel as I was going through a lot of the tragedy in the trials within my journey.

Starting a business seems complex, but it doesn't have to be. There are simple ways to approach the process, and I know that having something of your own will be fulfilling. You have full control over your destiny. You have the opportunity to change other people's lives. It's also an opportunity to give back to society and create a legacy. These things can help you achieve mental and emotional resilience. There are ten items you need to start your entrepreneurial journey.

Resilient Moments

What You Need to Start

1. A strong and polished business name
2. A logo
3. A mission and vision statement
4. A website and all social media networks
5. Determine whether to become an LLC (limited liability company) or an Inc. (corporation)
6. A business model
7. Marketing plan and strategy
8. An accountant/tax preparer and access to an attorney
9. A business bank account
10. Media kit/bio

These items are simple to obtain and give you a foundation to start the process. Starting out, I didn't know about the majority of these items on this list, which led me to losing out on many opportunities. So, when we talk about losing, I've lost many business deals over the years, and I have encountered some really grimy and unethical people. I didn't equip myself with the right information, business acumen, or data with some of these losses. I believe some of the business failings were my fault. I could have been more aggressive as far as seeking information, verifying, and not trusting so much. All of these realizations come with experience and self-discovery. But I've also learned that you can't cry over spilled milk. I've learned that you have to take the good with the bad. Some deals will come and be amazing, smooth sailing, and other deals will fall apart. I have some great working relationships with people at various networks and record labels. I am blessed and I thank God for those relationships.

There is plenty of solid advice I would give to anyone embarking upon their own entrepreneurial journey whether in music, entertainment, or any other field. You get what you negotiate. Let me repeat: YOU GET WHAT YOU NEGOTIATE. To trust but verify and seek additional information. Oftentimes in business, as women, we're too trusting and accommodating. You don't want to not trust people, but you want to investigate and verify that the information they're giving you is accurate and correct. This protects you and protects your emotional well-being. I think one big lesson that I've learned, just looking back after suffering a stillbirth, losing a baby, and getting breast cancer, is that life still goes on, and that means your business must go on. Your business still has to move forward, and you have to find a balance between healing yourself and running a business. When you figure this balance out, you win. This is what makes you resilient.

My entertainment business journey was not easy. It was riddled with failures and successes. I've lost out on some pretty big opportunities, which could have led to six-figure payouts. There was a business deal I failed to secure in 2014 because I trusted the people involved too much. This created a huge financial loss for Syleena and me. It wasn't inexperience that created this bad business move, but poor judgment on my part and poor character on theirs. In the end, we ended up solidifying something better in its place, but a loss like this could have broken me, especially since it came right after losing my baby.

On the other hand, I've closed some pretty impressive deals. Over the last twenty years, I've solidified, booked, and closed nearly six million in business deals. From securing record label deals from Universal Music, Shanachie Records, and eOne Nashville, to over thirty television deals and appearances for my clients. I've worked with many brands, promoters, and agents to book tours and festivals. I've been able to secure five South African tours, European tours, and US tours by myself. I've closed book deals and movie deals. I've created and arranged speaking tours for myself and my clients. One of my most impactful projects was working with The Christian Dion Collection, an inspirational apparel line. I secured a partnership for it with aspireTV and the aspireTV marketplace. So, for every deal lost there was always a better and bigger deal closed in its place. This is resilience.

Everybody's journey with entrepreneurship is different. For me, it was starting something that I knew nothing about back in 2002. When I entered the entertainment business, I was very naive. I learned everything on my own. I had no mentors. Over time I started to realize that this was how it was going to be for me as an entrepreneur: I was going to have to learn things on my own. I was going to have to take the tough road. But as an educator and a professor with three degrees, I knew I had all the tools and skills needed to be successful. I've coached close to a thousand people and educated more than 8,000 students and trained 200 entrepreneurs. I've traveled the world, I've built brands for people, and I've helped people build their businesses. I feel good about where I am right now today, so this chapter is for you to think about either leaving the rat race or starting something new as a part of your healing and resilience journey.

CHAPTER 7
More Money, No Problems

M*oney can buy happiness if spent the right way.*
No one becomes successful without sacrifice. Success and money are often spoken of in the same sentence, but they are not the same. My relationship with money has evolved over the years. I don't think people talk enough about money and resilience. I have filed for bankruptcy. I've bought a home. I've had to sell that home through a short sale. I've had tons of apartments and I've been close to eviction. I've made six figures for the past fifteen years, but I haven't been the best as it relates to money. Some people think more money, more problems. I disagree. I think the more money you have should be looked at from a lens of having fewer problems in certain areas of your life.

People tend to have a toxic relationship with money. I know I have had one. Having money is a privilege that we all should be afforded in this world. Money can buy happiness if spent the right way. Yes, I will repeat that. Money can buy happiness. It eliminates financial anxiety. It allows you to have better healthcare and get a good education. It also allows you to obtain experiences that lead to happiness such as vacations, visits to memorable places, and the opportunity to ensure a stable and productive life for your children, which may build upon your resilience factor. It creates a sense of freedom and calmness.

But wealth alone is not freedom or prosperity. Prosperity should be defined as what you believe prosperity to be. You can have a million dollars and not feel prosperous in your soul because you suffer from other internal demons or traumas. You can have $1,000 in your bank account and feel prosperous and rich. Prosperity is not defined as successful in material terms, but flourishing financially, mentally, and emotionally. Let's look at the concept of material things or terms. If I think back on when I lost my baby, if she would have survived I most likely would have felt prosperous in my spirit because I was a mother and would spend the next eighteen-plus years raising a child I wanted very much. That is prosperity to me. Again, living breast-cancer-free right now allows me to feel prosperous in my spirit. I don't think prosperity should be tied solely to financial worth or financial gain. Prosperity can be a mindset, too. Prosperity for each person is different.

One of the most prosperous years of my life was 2007, when I made well over six figures. I was single, free, just bought a new car, and I had my townhome. I was living my best life. I thought I was on top of the world. I was living it up and making major moves with my business and clients. I had lots of extra income coming in, and I just felt really good. Let's fast-forward to 2008; I lost it all. I had to pack up and leave Chicago to find new momentum. I got a great teaching opportunity in New York City, and I drove my car across the country to teach in the fall of 2008. I had to rebuild and start over. For many people, this would break them. For me, I found it to be a challenge to conquer a new obstacle. Don't get me wrong, I got tired of starting over, losing and gaining, but I realized early on, my journey would be different. From a financial standpoint, I started over several times in my life, and I've had to rebuild more than I can imagine. Prosperity fluctuates, therefore we must take measured steps to maintain a thoughtful balance through life. We should never get cocky or complacent because one minute you could be on top of the world and the next minute you could hit rock bottom. Learning to adjust, grow, and pick yourself up is the greatest skill you can have.

I have learned that there are three types of income you should obtain in life: active income, passive income, and portfolio income. These types of income are critical to surviving in this new economy that we live in. Active income is your salaries and wages from services you perform that involves active participation. Passive income is income you earn without actively being involved; this money is made while you sleep. Imagine making money while you sleep. That's a beautiful thing. Portfolio income is income derived from stocks, real estate, or investments in bonds. Also, imagine going through trauma, tragedy, and tribulations and not having the financial means to survive. Healthcare is expensive; gym memberships are expensive, too. Investing in therapy, self-help books, and self-care massage, all of these things cost money. So yes, we do need money, but money should not define us. Money should not be the ultimate deciding factor if we can bounce back or recover. Resilience is free. Resilience has no financial cost to it because it's a mindset.

After losing my baby, I went on maternity leave and disability. If it wasn't for having my own business, I would not have survived on disability payments solely. This tragedy is the moment I realized entrepreneurship is a must in today's society. If I didn't have extra income, I don't think I would have survived most of the things that I encountered after that. I was able to pour back into myself through self-care, such as massages, spa visits, and state-of-the-art gym facilities, and investing in myself by attending and speaking at conferences and expos around the country. I was also able to see a therapist for years at a time. Many people do not have this luxury. So, this chapter is all about giving you some tools from a financial standpoint to help with the way you deal with trauma. This chapter is about giving you some skills and a little empowerment from a financial standpoint that will enable you to bounce back and recover and be more resilient.

While I was working on my mental and physical state after I lost the baby, I created an income model for me and my clients to live by. I call it my 5-E Model. It's based on the principle that you can make money based on what you know. I have gained an immense amount of knowledge over my life span, and leveraging this would be critical to my growth process. I believe everyone needs at least three to four income streams to live comfortably. In today's society, you may even need seven!

I created an income-creation blueprint that I live by. This model helped me get through some very trying times in my life, as related to my finances, while I was going through some of the toughest setbacks that a person could face, losing a baby, breast cancer, bad breakups, and much more. So what this model does is it looks at you as a person and what you know, and then it asks the question: How can you leverage your education, experience, expertise, empowerment, and the economy in order to make passive or active income? The active income is something that we have to actually be involved in. Passive income is our key to ultimate success financially and for prosperity.

Below you will see the model, and you should answer the questions in order. Think and reflect about where you stand in life as it relates to your finances. The first part of this model is focused on education. I had to evaluate my education. I looked at what degrees I have obtained, certificates earned, and other professional development activities I've participated in. I realized as a consultant, coach, and educator I can make money in a particular field or industry. I had to really look at the education I've obtained and how I was using it. Was I using it to the best of my ability? Was I making money with the skills I have obtained and the degrees I earned?

There was a mindset shift I had to make. When you are faced with trauma or certain experiences, you learn to evaluate your life in its totality. When you're faced with ongoing disability or some other kind of setback, your response is crucial. Now the colleges that I've taught at were very supportive through all of my difficult times, but still I couldn't rely on them. I had to develop a plan that wouldn't leave me broke and destitute.

I want people to look at their education, experiences, and then evaluate your expertise based on how you are leveraging these things. Do you have any skills or abilities that you could use that would allow you to consult, train, or speak? Also, I began to do more speaking. I had to get out there and tell my story. This is another way to make money through the concept of empowering others. Not only was I sharing my story with other people and other women that have gone through similar situations, but I was finding new ways to bring in income. I learned early on in my life that pain pays. I don't mean that in an aggressive and cutthroat way. I mean we should turn our pain into our purpose and ultimately get paid for it. Sometimes we are able to help someone else get through their brutal situation and heal their pain through our pain, so it becomes a win-win type of situation.

I was sharing my story. When I was on the stage speaking, part of me was healing myself while simultaneously helping and healing others. Another aspect of my 5-E Model is for people to look at the economy and figure out ways to tap into other industries. We are now living through a pandemic, and this crisis is teaching us that we must be resilient and prepared. This is a perfect example of studying the economy and seeing these layoffs as a sign of where the jobs will be in the future. Where is the growth? What's next? So, you have to think about this as it relates to you, your journey, and your financial freedom. It's your turn to work on my 5-E income creation model and explore various ways that you can earn income and make money. Again, remember it's not about being rich or wealthy, it's about freedom and that is financial freedom. Understand that more money does not equal more problems. More money gives you freedom for financial security and future preparation. The more you prepare yourself mentally, spiritually, physically, and financially, the better off you are to be resilient and recover from anything life throws at you.

Resilient Moments

Creating New Income Streams

How can you leverage your education, experience, expertise, and the economy in order to make passive and active income?

Your education: What degrees have you obtained? Can you become a consultant in a particular field? List your education.

Your experience: What type of jobs have you held? Can you become an independent contractor? Launch a website in a particular area?

Your expertise: Do you have any skills, abilities, or expertise that allows you to consult, teach, speak, write, or develop a website in that profession?

Your empowerment capacity: Can you teach, speak, or write?

The economy: Are there any booming jobs and/or careers in today's economy that you could capitalize off of?

When I was at my lowest point in life, I had to figure out a way to keep making money and earning income through it all. The goal of this exercise is for you to generate ideas surrounding income stream creation that we sometimes overlook. Oftentimes, we feel we need more education or training; that is not always the case. We usually have either education or experience that we have acquired over the years that could be immediately turned into an idea or business concept. This also works with product development. You should think of products that you could sell or add to your business repertoire. It's simple and an effective way to add extra income without the extra work. I believe your mental, physical, emotional, social, and financial mindset must be in order to bounce back or recover from life's tragedy. It's one thing to go through trauma and another thing to go through it broke or financially unstable. It adds more hurt and pain to the situation.

Oftentimes, I feel as if people forget about the financial component to survival and how it impacts their ability to be resilient. How can you be whole if financially you are suffering? How can you be strong if, financially, you can't afford your medication or pills or just to go to the doctor? Therapy is not free or cheap. For most people, copays still exist in this world we live in. We don't have a free healthcare system, so we have to take a look at our financial well-being and what we view as being prosperous and the role it plays in our resilience.

I'd like to share with you how I view resilience and success. Looking back on my life, I know that I've suffered a lot. I've gone through a lot. I've also been very successful in many areas of my life. I measure success in a very different way from what other people may think success looks like. Success is an attitude. It's when you've done everything you could to accomplish your goals, but still come up short and still push through to achieve them by accepting your failures. Your success will look different from everyone else's. Your goal in life should be to prove yourself to yourself, not others.

We all have different finish lines that we complete throughout this race. With these facts in mind, you can define what your success looks like. There are no rules. Success is an idea that is often misconstrued by those who do not know the true meaning of the word. I wish more people would look at it as an accomplishment of an aim, goal, or purpose. I believe that if people looked at success that way, it would help them navigate through life. Stop comparing your success with others. The most resilient people would probably say that their success is not determined by money or fame, but by the impact that they have made on others. Everyone's success varies and will look different because of the different lives we live. We all have different dreams and aspirations in life that when accomplished make us successful. I want you to know about success and how simple we should approach it.

Resilient Moments

Simple Facts about Success

1. In order to be successful, you must have a written plan. Your plan must include goals/objectives, be organized, specific, and well thought out.

2. Success is defined by you. No one else can measure your success. It's based on what you want to accomplish. If making six figures a year is your idea of success, and you complete that goal, you are successful.

3. Success does not include complacency. Success is about constantly reaching new goals and reaching new heights. In life we have a greater purpose, which is to keep achieving and moving.

4. Success is about action. You have to do the work. But more importantly, do the work that brings you joy and challenges you.

5. The most successful people study, read, research, and prepare. They are in their respective fields and industries learning and growing. They evolve and push themselves to continue achieving their goals.

And finally, I've developed some principles and values that I live by. I call them my "Success Factor Keys." I read these daily. They are on my vision board. Reading these to myself out loud every day serves as a constant reminder that I can achieve anything, I can bounce back from anything, and that success is a mindset.

Resilient Moments

Keys to Your Success

1. Keep the faith and execute your ideas.
2. Dream big and bold!
3. Trust one person-yourself.

4. Stay in your lane.
5. Don't give your ideas away too early.
6. Visualize success!
7. Invest in yourself.
8. Master your work ethic.
9. Out innovate the competition.
10. Be pleasant, but stand firm on what you believe in.
11. We have to develop financial resilience as well to live a healthy, free, and successful life.

Resilient Moments

Developing Financial Resilience

1. Have an emergency fund with three times your monthly income.
2. Invest in the stock market.
3. Make sure you have all of your insurance in order: life, health, auto, and business insurance.
4. Limit your debt.
5. Build your assets: real estate, intellectual property, and other items that appreciate in value.
6. Create social capital, the ability to work with others in social groups.
7. Change your mindset about money.
8. Focus on being wealthy, not rich.
9. Learn to love whatever you have in your bank account.
10. Learn to deal with failure.

CHAPTER 8

A Purposeful Pandemic

Nothing can prepare you for a global pandemic.
For my final chapter, I thought it would be interesting to take you inside my latest test. Currently, we're in the midst of a pandemic the whole world is facing. In March of 2020, the world stopped. COVID-19 took over our lives and put the world into self-isolation or, as some would call it, a quarantine. It's funny because I didn't think life could get any worse from surviving a stillbirth or beating breast cancer, but here comes 2020, full of hand sanitizer, face masks, and social distancing. I told you life was unpredictable. You never know what it's going to throw at you. Now, we are dealing with this latest traumatic event. We're forced to focus like a laser on health and wellness, in addition to our mental sanity.

Living through a pandemic has been full of uncertainty. And it's hard to stay focused when the news is overwhelming in its reporting of the ongoing issues the world is facing because of the pandemic. For me, this coronavirus health crisis has been full of emotional highs and lows. At the start of the pandemic, I ended a relationship. A breakup isn't easy, but it's even harder to endure virtually. Therefore, I was forced to start therapy. I started virtual therapy to deal with some of the emotional setbacks that these drastic turns of events forced me to deal with. Resilience is also about understanding when you need help. I had suffered several anxiety attacks and mental breakdowns, so I wanted to make sure I was doing everything possible to keep my hormones balanced, stress low, and mind right. There was a situation where I passed out from mental stress and dehydration. I was doing my best to not get overwhelmed with sudden changes to my life, but 2020 brought on new challenges.

On a positive note, I started on my book during this pandemic. I began an extreme amount of self-discovery, self-reflection, and mental cleansing. During this pandemic, I've been faced with some severe personal issues in my relationships as well as financial setbacks. My entrepreneurial ventures were affected severely; half of my income was wiped out with this pandemic because the world stopped. No music, no concerts, and entertainment came to a halt. I really mean 50 percent. It was devastating and ridiculous. When you work in entertainment a lot of your income comes from concerts, because I would get commissions from tours and events. These tours and events stopped. I had many speaking engagements set up for 2020, which all had to be canceled because of the pandemic. However, this time I decided to do something different and tap into my creativity and innovation. I already had a business model built on several income streams, which allowed me to revamp and shift quickly.

The day my college decided to shift from on-site classes to online classes because of the coronavirus was the day I booked my flight to Atlanta, Georgia.

It's almost like I predicted what was to come. I flew to Atlanta to stay with my sister Syleena, and it turned into an interesting and an exhilarating time. I stayed with her family and my friends, and we made the best of it. That's all you can do in these kinds of uncertain times. From experiencing the jarring, emotional hit of having to put so many things on hold and reevaluating opportunities, coming to Atlanta put my mindset back on track.

In addition to the pandemic, our country faced racial unrest with the killing of George Floyd. Within a three month period, black people were confronted with the brutal killings of Breonna Taylor, Ahmaud Arbury, Rayshard Brooks and others. Social media displayed these videos for the world to see thus causing more trauma for many in the black community. There was a moment in 2020 that I felt as if things could not get worse as I watched cities burn and protestors in the streets fighting for justice. The pandemic which brought about more people in poverty and racial injustices weighed heavy on me. I prayed daily for God to change the trajectory of our country.

Although I found myself facing many stressful events both directly and indirectly, I used the opportunity to grow and focus that growth on being a better human being. I'm learning about myself each day. I am finding out some things I like about myself and other things I don't like about myself. I want to use the time to correct those things I don't like. I'm learning to be gentle with myself. I'm also learning not to be so hard on myself. There's been a lot of self-discovery and reflection during this pandemic, and it's just another testament to what I can overcome.

Surviving and thriving are both necessary. Something I've asked myself recently is what's next? How can I jump-start this moment onto the next? What can I do to grow and improve myself? After I lost seventy pounds, I often wondered, should I lose more? For many women, these questions are constantly thought about and contemplated. Right now, we often find ourselves wondering about the next step after this pandemic is over. For some people, they may not think of the next step in this way, feeling like they are confident enough to succeed in all their endeavors or resilient enough to bounce back. Many people have lost jobs, income, and much more, so it may not be that easy. This pandemic took the lives of so many, and it is really a time of reflection. I think about all of the families affected by COVID-19 and how they now have to tap into their resilience factor. We should all strive for living in our truth, being our best selves, and practicing good health and wellness. I know my goal in life is to survive and thrive.

Resilient Moments

Ways to Move toward Surviving and Thriving

1. Eliminate negative people from your circle. Let go of people who do not allow you the space to grow, bring happiness to your life, and hinder you from truly being able to get to that next step.
2. Eliminate things that no longer serve you. If it doesn't bring you joy, you shouldn't keep it in your life.

3. Eliminate the "I can't" mindset. If you start your day in a negative way, how likely are you to reach your goals? Don't set yourself up for failure if you haven't tried yet.
4. Focus on things you love, business or personal. If you love to work out, go to the gym. Put your passions into motion.
5. Lay out a plan. Most people fail to plan. Though we do have time, it's important to plan to know exactly what you need to do next to accomplish your goals.

Ultimately if you wake up asking yourself what's next, it's up to you to answer it. For the rest of your life it's important to refocus and shift your mindset. With new challenges and obstacles ahead of us, you should be evolving with each moment. Life is never stagnant, so you shouldn't be either. Each test is different from the last, and that should be taken as an opportunity for you to grow and develop good character, a strong mindset, and an unbreakable spirit. In taking care of yourself, mind and body, you must shift your mindset to positive beliefs and habits that allow this growth to manifest.

Resilient Moments

Embracing change and shifting your mindset

1. Meditate more. Meditation is the best way to clear your mind and become centered.
2. Train your mind to wake up positively. The way you wake up sets your intention and tone for

the day. If you wake up with negative thoughts, then the rest of your day will be negative.

3. Journaling (I can't stress this enough): writing down thoughts, ideas, and feelings is a great way to clear your thoughts. With your mind cleared, you can shift your mindset to priorities and goals.

4. Imagine the inevitable. Think bigger, think outside of the box. Everything that has been done in the world started as impossible ideas before being executed and created. Eliminate the failure mindset. We don't lose, we learn. We don't fail, we find new ways of doing things successfully.

Embrace the world around you. It's impossible to change your mindset and embrace change if you aren't learning about the world around you. I want to travel more, go to new places and museums after this pandemic ends. We should all get out of our comfort zone to experience new things. We should do more things that will help our mind and body. Exercising regularly, doing yoga, going for runs or walks will boost your endorphins, ultimately making you feel better.

Embracing the world and all of its changes starts with you. How you start your day, what you learn, and how you take care of yourself all play a key part in shifting your mindset. Every day, and even every moment, you have the ability to choose how you make the most of your life. We must be grateful for the challenges and thankful for the ability to overcome them. The obstacles you encounter are meant to make you learn and grow, testing your resiliency. Life will test you before it will bless you. Don't expect to be perfect or permanent. We are all a work in progress just trying to conquer this thing called life! I wanted to use this pandemic to find further purpose for my life. Remember, everything that happens to you prepares you and builds your resilience factor.

Experience is the greatest teacher. I have learned that forgiveness of myself and others was essential to my well-being. When you forgive you heal, and when you let go, you grow. You grow stronger and more resilient with each day that passes. I will say this, you never know what life will bring you, so always be prepared to embrace the good and the bad that comes your way. I wanted to share with you my last test before you start working on your own self-discovery by completing the *Resilience Journal* at the end of this book.

Your Resilience Factor Journal

Self-Discovery

Write a short essay to your younger self.

_____

_____

_____

_____

_____

_____

_____

_____

_____

_____

_____

_____

_____

_____

_____

_____

_____

Identify ten positive qualities you have discovered about yourself.

1. _____

2. _____

3. _____

4. _____

5. _____

6. _____

7. _____

8. _____

9. _____

10. _____

Identify ten negative qualities you have discovered about yourself.

1. _____

2. _____

3. _____

4. _____

5. _____

6. _____

7. _____

8. _____

9. _____

10. _____

What do you want in life?

_____

_____

_____

_____

_____

What makes you happy?

_____

_____

_____

_____

_____

Are you fearful of discovering your weaknesses? Explain why you answered, "yes," "no," or "unsure."

_____

_____

_____

_____

_____

_____

_____

What is your definition of self-love?

_____

_____

_____

_____

_____

_____

_____

Identify your core values. What do you believe in?

_____

_____

_____

_____

_____

_____

_____

How often do you celebrate yourself?

_____

_____

_____

_____

_____

_____

_____

What are your daily struggles?

_____

_____

_____

_____

_____

_____

_____

How do you cope with life's stress?

_____

_____

_____

_____

_____

_____

_____

Dr. Syleecia Thompson

What triggers cause you to lose hope or faith?

_____

_____

_____

_____

_____

_____

_____

What is your reaction to these triggers?

_____

_____

_____

_____

_____

_____

_____

How often do you take responsibility for hurting yourself or others? Explain.

_____

_____

_____

_____

_____

_____

_____

What makes you smile?

_____

_____

_____

_____

_____

_____

Name two moments in your life you will never forget. Describe them in detail and identify what makes them unforgettable.

_____

_____

_____

_____

_____

_____

_____

What surprises you most about your life?

_____

_____

_____

_____

_____

_____

_____

How do you know when you have had enough? What is your breaking point?

_____

_____

_____

_____

_____

_____

_____

Write the words you need to hear at this moment in your life?

_____

_____

_____

_____

_____

_____

_____

Spiritual Resilience

Spiritual Resilience is defined as the ability to sustain an individual's sense of self and purpose through a set of beliefs, principles, or values. Spiritual Resilience can be built on four pillars. They are perseverance, purpose, perspective, and a higher power. Build your spiritual foundation below using these four pillars.

Perseverance (What keeps you going when things look bad?)

_____

_____

_____

_____

_____

Purpose (What keeps you grounded, connected, and focused. This is your why.)

_____

_____

_____

_____

_____

Perspective (How will you view trauma or tragedy going forward?)

_____

_____

_____

_____

_____

_____

_____

Higher Power (Define the higher power you utilize as a source of resilience.)

_____

_____

_____

_____

_____

_____

_____

How to Increase Your Resilience (Quantity)

Increasing resilience is centered around quantity. Here are five ways to increase resilience. Read and reflect.

1. Build a community of support.
2. Start a wellness program (exercise daily, nutrition, and sleep at least six to eight hours).
3. Meditate daily.
4. Invest in yourself.
5. Know your limits.

Reflection:

_____

_____

_____

_____

_____

_____

_____

_____

_____

How to Build Resilience (Quality)

Building resilience is centered on quality. Here are five ways to build resilience. Read and reflect.

1. Avoid seeing crises as undefeatable problems.
2. Accept that change is a part of living.
3. Nurture an optimistic view of yourself.
4. Take decisive actions. Be deliberate.
5. Take care of yourself.

Reflection:

_____

_____

_____

_____

_____

_____

_____

_____

_____

Dr. Syleecia Thompson

Your Resilience Factor

Congratulations! You've made it to the end of this book. Healing is part of your journey. Resilience is your superpower. Now is your moment to create your resilience factor. Demonstrating resiliency doesn't necessarily mean you haven't suffered difficulty or distress. It also doesn't mean you haven't experienced emotional pain or sadness. The road to resilience is often paved with emotional stress and strain. However, we all have the tools within us to recover, release, and remove that which holds us back. We must understand who we are and how we operate. We must challenge ourselves every day to never give up on ourselves. We must fight. We must continue to tell ourselves that we can overcome any tragedy or trauma. The moment you start believing that you can bounce back is the same moment you realize that things will all work out. Your belief is everything. You can learn to be more resilient. You can practice through positive affirmations and your written commitment. Positive affirmations help us to build resilience. The following positive statements should be read daily. Repeat these statements out loud in the mirror every morning:

I am strong.
I am powerful.
I am loved.
I am smart.
I will get all that my heart desires.
I am enough.

Your written commitment is to create your resilience factor statement. Finish the following sentence: I will navigate any crisis, trauma, or tragedy by:

_____

_____

_____

_____

_____

_____

Reflection:

_____

_____

_____

_____

_____

_____

_____

_____

_____

I had such an awesome time in college. This was the day me and my sorority sisters competed in our first step show at SIUE.

College Days at SIUE with my Sorority Sisters.

A week after my breast cancer surgery. I felt empowered.

A fun experience touring with Kanye West, John Legend, Syleena and GLC in Europe for The College Dropout Tour.

Dr. Syleecia Thompson

Being honored for 10 years of teaching at Berkeley College in NYC.

Catholic School Picture day. I went to St. John the Baptist from grades 1 through 5.

Discipline and Determination, 70lb weight loss.

I took swimming lessons as a child but I still can't swim!

College days at SIUE. I had a blast!

Family pictures were always a special memory.

I attended an event with former president of Pepisco, Indra Nooyi. Amazing experience!

Me, my sister Sylette and my Dad.

I was born on Christmas Day. This was one of my birthday parties.

My family with Iyanla Vanzant. Fix My Life was a life-changing experience for me.

In Washington, D.C. for Zeta Phi Beta
Centennial Celebration.

My sisters and I. Syleena doing her homework!

Meeting Mr. Knowles. A legend in the music business.

My mom and I at my childhood home in Harvey, IL.

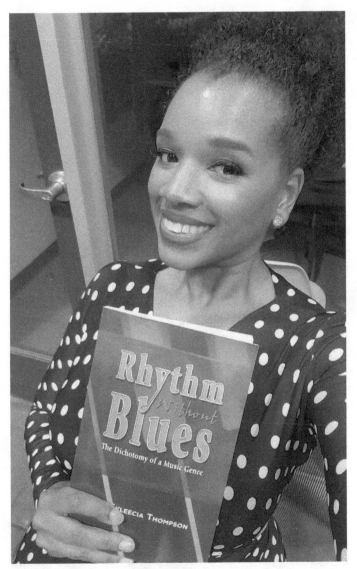

My first book, Rhythm without Blues!

Michael Jordan at my 31st birthday. My cousin and I shared a moment with him.

This is the day I graduated from High School.

My first procedure in preparation for my Lumpectomy.

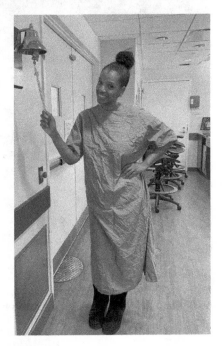

The day I finished my radiation therapy! I rang the bell. The best day ever.

My grandfather. This was the last picture I took of him before he passed away. He was an amazing man.

My sisters and my mom. My best friends.

The day I found out I was
pregnant in Amsterdam.

Syleena's album release event with record label eOne Nashville reps Gina Miller and Omega.

Nobody knew I had a radiation session after this speaking engagement. I was in pain the entire time. It was a moment.

The Best Me Conference in Oakland, CA.

Speaking at a Women's Conference in Lesotho, Africa.

The site where Nelson Mandela was captured in South Africa.

The place where Nelson Mandela voted for the first time after being captured. Historical moment for me after battling breast cancer.

This picture was right before I started radiation therapy. I attended The Boss Network's 10th Anniversary Conference.

About the Author

Dr. Syleecia Thompson is an entertainment manager, professor, author, brand strategist, and executive producer. She takes a multifaceted approach to entrepreneurship, considering herself The Serial Entrepreneur. Her company focuses on empowerment, entertainment, entrepreneurship, and education. She has launched and led over 200 master classes, taught more than 8,000 students globally, solidified and booked more than $6,000,000 in television, book, music, concert, and film deals. Her skills also include producing, coordinating, overseeing, and launching events and book releases for herself and several clients. Her client list includes Grammy-nominated singer, actress, and talk show host Syleena Johnson, transformation coach and wellness expert Dr. Ivan Hernandez, board-certified dermatologist and entrepreneur Dr. Dele-Michael, and large and small companies in various industries. Some of her projects include eleven nationally released albums, an independent record label, reality shows, a BET film, tours, empowerment events, book tours, talk shows, media and television tours, entrepreneur coaching programs, and much more. Recently she launched her own production company, Dr. Syleecia Productions, and it became the home of two projects, *The Making of a Woman* documentary on Fox Soul, and *The Startup*, a digital series on CleoTV. She's worked on projects with companies such as Shanachie Records, Sony/RCA/Jive, Universal, BET, TV One, Aspire, The Grace Institute, The Survivor Movement, Essence, Think Factory Media, and Universal Attractions. She's booked her clients on *The Doctors, R&B Divas, Sister Circle*, ABC, CBS, Fox, TV One, BET, *Marriage Boot Camp, Fix My Life, L.A. Hair, Maury Povich,* and many more. With several successful tours under her belt in Africa, Europe, North America, and Canada, she still dedicates herself to a focused and concentrated business model: vision leads the way.

She is also a speaker and published author. Her book *Rhythm Without Blues: The Dichotomy of a Music Genre* was released in 2010 and focused on R&B music. Dr. Syleecia is a writer who has produced content for the *Encyclopedia of African-American Music*, which included her essays for the Chicago music scene from 1948 to the present. She currently runs a 150-person Entrepreneur Network called The Visionaries, where she coaches, trains, and supports women and men entrepreneurs. As a full-time professor, she teaches undergraduate and graduate students in the areas of management, leadership, change, global business, entrepreneurship, music management, and various business topics. She is an advocate for pregnancy loss, health, wellness, and fitness due to her recent seventy-pound weight loss success story after suffering a devastating pregnancy loss at seven months. She is passionate about sharing her message and journey with the world with her motto "Vision. Plan. Execute." Her dedication and determination to reap excellence and results for her clients, authors, and business associates will be undeniable and unmatched in this ever-changing economy.

CPSIA information can be obtained
at www.ICGtesting.com
Printed in the USA
BVHW080603300321
603653BV00005B/835